FIGURAL

Napkin Rings

Collector's Identification and Value Guide

Lillian Gottschalk
Sandra Whitson

COLLECTOR BOOKS
A Division of Schroeder Publishing Co., Inc.

On the cover:
Rip Van Winkle, Plate 345; Cherub with flute, Plate 430; Cat with glass eyes, Plate 1.

Book Design: Karen Long
Cover Design: Karen Geary

Additional copies of this book may be ordered from:

COLLECTOR BOOKS
P.O. Box 3009
Paducah, KY 42002-3009

@$18.95. Add $2.00 for postage and handling.

Copyright: Lillian Gottschalk and
Sandra Whitson, 1996

CONTENTS

Acknowledgments *4*

Introduction *5*

Animals — Domestic *8*

    Cats *8*

    Dogs *13*

    Combinations with Cats and Dogs *31*

    Cows and Bulls *36*

    Goats *38*

    Horses and Donkeys *40*

    Sheep *46*

Animals — Wild *48*

    Bears *48*

    Deer *49*

    Foxes and Wolves *54*

    Lions *58*

    Mice and Rats *59*

    Monkeys *61*

    Rabbits *65*

    Squirrels *69*

    Miscellaneous *76*

Birds *81*

    Large, Small, Long-tailed Birds,
        Cockatoos and Eagles *81*

    Roosters, Hens, and Geese *107*

    Cranes, Storks, Swans, and Herons . . .*114*

    Owls *118*

Bud Vases *123*

Chairs and Stools *136*

Characters *139*

Combination Sets *147*

Cherubs and Cupids *175*

    With Wings *175*

    Without Wings *186*

Fans, Butterflies, Flowers, Fruits, and Berries *194*

Kate Greenaway Types *207*

    Infants *207*

    Boys *208*

    Girls *216*

    Combinations of Girls and Boys *229*

    Women *235*

Marine Life *237*

    Beavers *237*

    Dolphins *238*

    Frogs *239*

    Shells *242*

    Turtles *243*

Military *245*

Miscellaneous Subjects *248*

People *260*

    Boys *260*

    Girls *275*

    Men *278*

    Women *283*

Sports *287*

Fakes, Mistakes, and Mysteries *296*

Catalog Pages and Reference Materials .*318*

Manufacturers and Merchandisers . . .*346*

Photo Credits *346*

Bibliography *347*

Index *349*

About the Authors *351*

ACKNOWLEDGMENTS

While the majority of American, Victorian figural napkin rings shown in this book are from the collections of the authors, there are a number of individuals to thank for their assistance and willingness to share their collections, libraries, catalogs, and knowledge. A book like this arises out of the shared interests of many persons. Without them, this book would not have been possible. A great debt of gratitude is due the following: Meta Bleier, Anne Crowe, Louise Goodman, Dr. H. William Gottschalk, Robert H. Harper, Sheila and Russ Harrington, Stanley and Irma Jacobson, S. Barbara Klausner, Rosemarie LaBelle, Lillian Markey, Lauren Mekalian, Ruth Mosunic, Chuck Patterson, Jack Podner, Bill Purdue, Charlotte and Vance Underhill, and Peter Unitt.

We are particularly indebted to collectors-dealers, Ron and Joyce Bronow, two of our main contributors who loaned us photographs taken by Ron when interesting and unusual napkin rings passed through their hands. These napkin rings were no longer available for re-photographing. We also appreciate information supplied by the Bronows, which was necessary for identification of these photographs. Ron also gave to us photographs that he took of important material from the archives of The International Silver Co..

Special credit is extended to Steve and Barbara Aaronson, who provided photographs of a few rarities from their collection and also from collections of others. Steve's knowledge of figural napkin rings exceeds the ordinary, and he has been very generous in sharing helpful information.

Our appreciation is extended to the lovely lady in Baltimore who we met for the very first time and allowed us to borrow napkin rings we needed for photographing. For her trust and help, we owe our thanks. She wishes to remain anonymous.

Another contributor was a lady in New York City, who also wishes to remain anonymous and who allowed two strangers into her home to examine and document a number of rare, figural napkin rings. To her we extend a special thanks.

The late Diana Cramer, past editor of *Silver Magazine*, will always be remembered for her encouragement of this project and permission to use the Reed & Barton catalog pages, which had been reproduced in the magazine.

To the gentlemen from Virginia, who loaned us the monkey band napkin rings for photographing, we owe a special thanks for their trust and appreciate their generosity. Their collection contains a greater number of monkey-musician napkin rings than we have seen before.

Significant information was also provided by Bernice Morehouse of the Meriden Historical Society in Meriden, Connecticut, who on one very rainy day pulled out of storage every manufacturer's catalog available at the time and allowed us to photograph the material that was needed for our research. The International Silver Co.'s archival material was turned over to the society when the archives were closed.

Last but truly first to us is Richard Goodbar, who photographed the majority of the napkin rings, put the manuscript on a computer, provided research material from his extensive library on the subject of silver, and acted as our mentor, tirelessly providing concepts and comments. Photographs contribute the greatest amount of information for a book of this type. So much work goes into positioning and lighting a napkin ring just right. In addition it takes special patience to photograph anything in silver. Richard was up to the task. Requests for retakes were graciously accepted. Often it was he who was dissatisfied and would insist on a new photograph. It was a pleasure to work with him, and the completed pictures speak for his talent. His wife Rosemary Goodbar is a walking encyclopedia, and we took advantage of her presence whenever possible. For all the time we took from the lives of the Goodbars, we give utmost thanks and love.

To all of the above and to any we may have inadvertently omitted, we are grateful.

Lillian Gottschalk

Sandra Whitson

The date when the first figural napkin rings were produced is uncertain, but for the most part they were mass produced between 1869 and the turn of the century. In 1867 a patent for napkin holders was granted. Combined along with the wide use of electroplating, the popularity of figural napkin rings introduced a whole new product line for many silver-plating companies.

American Victorian figural napkin rings have one thing in common; all are silver plated. Sterling figural napkin rings are generally British.

Victorians, who could not afford the cost of sterling, bought silver-plated items for the dining room. Dinner was a social event, a place to catch up on the happenings of the day and make future plans. The figural napkin rings were practical holders of cotton or linen napkins used over and over until time for the weekly wash.

The American companies of Meriden Britannia Co.; Simpson, Hall, Miller & Co.; and Acme Silver Co. established factories in Canada shortly after 1879 to avoid an import tariff imposed by the Canadian government to protect Canadian industry. The figural napkin rings produced in Canada by these companies were identical to those sold in the United States; however, new designs created specifically for the Canadian market, such as beavers, maple leaves, and the sport of curling, were added to the lines.

This book is not intended to be a history of companies that produced American silver-plated napkin rings. What has been attempted in this book is to document by means of photographs the immense variety of figural napkin rings produced by many companies. This book is a showcase of manufacturers' skills and abilities to market popular subjects, which reflect the beauty of figural napkin rings.

The names of the silver-plate manufacturers, which are employed in this book, are identified as they are found in original catalogs and advertisements.

The authors made a major effort to identify correctly the elusive makers who left no marks on their goods. While this has been the most difficult work of all—because of the scarcity of printed material on the subject—this book should provide a tool for those persons wary of the numerous figural napkin rings that are not marked.

In some instances, the marks are obscure or in an unusual location. This fact has been pointed out in the captions bringing to the buyers' attention the necessity to closely examine napkin rings for hidden marks.

Hours were spent checking and rechecking for fakes and reproductions and cross-checking manufacturers' numbers for authenticity. It was an education as this book slowly took shape. We learned much more than we could have imagined. For instance, we learned that some manufacturers' numbers followed a pattern while others used erratic sequences of numbers. This is particularly obvious with Wilcox Silver Plate Co. One of its numbering systems is a five-digit number that begins with a zero and is found with other makers' marks.

Silver-plate manufacturers bought and sold figures and bases from each other. The practice was common, although in most cases an effort was made to vary designs. Companies like Wilcox, Reed & Barton and Meriden Britannia Co. are known to have sold unplated figures and parts that were silver plated and marked by others in the trade.

Some of the silver-plate companies struggled with a depressed business climate that occurred during the last part of the 1900s. This problem, coupled with intense competition among the independent companies, gave impetus to the realization that a merger would be beneficial. In 1898 many of the companies agreed to merge, and The International Silver Co. was formed.

Times were changing fast, and the years just before World War I brought a change in lifestyle as well. The emergence of automobiles, buses, and trolleys along with road building meant transportation away from cities and into the suburbs. Life no longer centered in the city, and there were other attractions for busy people. Silver-plated napkin rings were a fashion that would fade.

Napkin rings with figures attached began to decline in popularity during the austere period imposed by World War I. During the Art Deco period, a simplicity of objects took place extending through the Great Depression, and Victorian figural napkin rings lost favor.

The 1950s inspired a revival of all things antique and drew buyers' attention to collecting cherished mementos from America's past. Gaining in favor from those years until now are the figural napkin rings, which are deemed table sculpture by some and enchanting table accessories by others. They are again appreciated for their design, workmanship, and subject matter. These items were made in an era when there was pride in workmanship. Many of the figural napkin rings show that much time and skill were taken in their creation.

As in Victorian days, these wonderful objects can start conversation at a table and exude the thrill they once commanded, especially when a subject is matched with the diner—made easy with the variety of napkin rings still available to buyers willing to seek them out.

It was impossible to include every figural napkin ring in existence. But the authors have attempted to select figural napkin rings that are illustrative of all the major categories and to incorporate a cross section of the commonly found napkin rings as well as the rare.

After considerable thought, it was decided to organize the contents of chapters according to the predominant figure or the major subject matter of the napkin ring. In fact, the division follows a pattern employed by a majority of collectors today. In some instances, there are napkin rings which embody two or more subjects. If in doubt, consult the index.

Grading & Pricing

Many factors were taken into consideration for grading the figural napkin rings. They include condition, rarity and demand as well as the quality of the casting. The grading used in this book is simply a guide. Prices will vary greatly in different areas and for a variety of reasons.

A—Few available. Rare. $500 and up.
B—Difficult to find. Highly collectible. $350 to $500.
C—Obtainable. $200 to $350.
D—Common or more readily obtainable. Under $200.

From A to D the rings are worth owning, and each has its own special attraction. Condition is a major factor for all of the grades. Missing parts or deep corrosion are the more serious defects. To many people, original, complete figural napkin rings that have not been replated are important contributions to their collections.

The selection of one type of figural napkin ring over another is a matter of personal taste. History informs us that if the ring was expensive when new, fewer were sold; therefore, fewer exist today. Or if it were a cheaper item that was not popular at its introduction, this too would be scarce today. All these circumstances are taken into consideration in determining the grading.

Prices are obsolete almost from the minute they are printed; therefore, the grading system with a range of values has been used to aid buyers. A plus sign (+) when added after a grade indicates the higher range of the price scale.

Silver Plating and Replating

A controversy exists today over whether or not to replate figural napkin rings. There is a group of collectors who are purists and feel that only untouched figural napkin rings are suitable for their collections. Replating can hide repairs, replacements, and patina that adds character to a ring. With all the fakes and forgeries surfacing today, it is a great worry to some that silver plating can hide reproductions, especially finely made ones.

On the other hand, many collectors wish to return the figural napkin rings to their original glory. Owners of napkin rings who wish to set the table with them are happier with a bright silver finish. Today, many silver platers are able to simulate an oxidized finish if desired. The bottom line on the subject of replating is simply a matter of personal taste.

Some replaters buff the finish too hard causing a loss of detail. Sculptural sharpness can disappear. Original engraving, embossing, and lines can lose definition. It is important to use a silver plater who will take the time to protect the napkin ring from irreparable damage and loss of value.

Manufacturers' Marks and Numbers

The most reliable and quickest way to identify napkin rings is to read the manufacturers' marks and numbers. Sometimes these marks are difficult to decipher because of wear, corrosion, or replating. On a few it has been observed that work on the ring—such as straightening and hammering—has damaged the marks and numbers.

A warning: Manufacturers' marks and numbers are currently being forged. Forgers read books, and extra care must now be taken for judgments on authenticities.

Makers' marks may take the form of coins (small disks, sometimes referred to as buttons), which are applied to the base and contain the manufacturers' name and/or trademark. They may also take the form of triangular, oval, or diamond-shaped appliqués. In some cases, these coins and appliques were necessary additions because of irregular surfaces or awkward areas, which made a strike (the makers' mark stamped with a die) impossible or difficult to execute.

Coins and appliqués were employed to cover a previous makers' mark, when the name of a company changed or when manufacturers purchased napkin rings from an original maker.

Coins are most prevalent on the napkin rings of Rogers & Brother; Simpson, Hall, Miller & Co.; and Meriden Britannia Co. However, these are the coins in use by fakers, so buyers beware.

Where identical napkin rings have the same number but different company names, it is generally because of a merger. For instance, a sitting hen is found marked Meriden Britannia Co. and an identical hen carries the name Rogers & Brother; however, both bear the same number 267. Rogers was acquired by Meriden in 1879. The Rogers' hen is earlier, but produced from the same casting.

While there may be more, only three times was it discovered that the manufacturer's catalog number differed from the number on the napkin ring. Perhaps the catalog contained a typographical error. However, when possible, manufacturers' names and numbers that are given in this book were taken from the actual napkin ring.

Wm. Rogers Mfg. Co. duplicated some numbers. One explanation is that these duplications may have occurred when the production of a napkin ring was closed out and the number re-used at a later date for a different napkin ring. For example, an early Rogers number 19 portrays a male child wearing a skirt, while the later version of Rogers number 19 features a Tom Sawyer-type figure that is clothed in trousers held up by suspenders.

Bolts and Wing Nuts

A few figural napkin rings have parts that are attached with bolts that drop into the base and are fastened with nuts or wing nuts. This allows parts to be removed for ease of cleaning.

Cats

Americans have long been intrigued by domestic cats' personalities. The subject of children's nursery rhymes and stories, the cat was an ideal theme for figural napkin rings, suitable for adults as well as children. Large and small figures of cats and kittens—doing things curious and playful—gave variety to the subject matter. Produced by many different manufacturers, cat figural napkin rings are collected by avid cat fanciers who claim cats with glass eyes as their favorites.

Pet Products News, an industry magazine, names cats as the most popular pet in the United States.

Plate 1

Meriden Britannia Co., Number 235. A very large, solid-cast cat with glass eyes carries a standard size napkin holder on its back. Grade B+, $350 – 500.

Plate 2

Left: *Maker and number not marked. (Located: Forbes Silver Co., number 1028.)* A large, contemplative cat sits by a napkin holder with a bead-and-reel edge. Grade C, $200 – 350. **Right:** *Meriden Britannia Co., Number 232.* A large, contemplative cat sits by a napkin holder on a plain, oval, ball-footed base. Grade B+, $350 – 500.

Plate 3

Knickerbocker Silver Co., Number 32. A small kitten rears up in a playful position, facing a napkin holder elevated by flowered supports. The raised rectangular base features a border of zigzags interspaced with half rosettes. Grade C, $200 – 350.

Plate 4

James W. Tufts, Number 1609. The cat with music stand has no napkin holder, but was designed for the napkin to rest in the open space. The sheet music carries the title "Over the Garden Wall," a song from the 1880s stage production *Ring Up the Curtain.* Grade B+, $350 – 500.

Plate 5

Left: *Maker and number not marked.* A medium-sized cat with glass eyes is positioned against a napkin holder. Grade C, $200 – 350. **Right:** *Rogers & Brother, Number 4337.* A cat with glass eyes sits on a round base facing a mouse. Grade C+, $200 – 350.

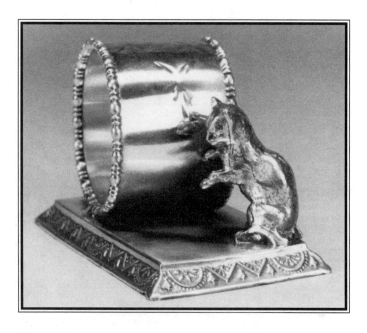

Plate 6

Knickerbocker Silver Co., Number 205. A small kitten sits on its hind legs alongside a bead-and-reel-edged napkin holder on a raised, rectangular base with a border of zigzags interspersed with half rosettes. Grade C, $200 – 350.

Plate 7

Maker and number not marked. A standing cat reaches for a fly on top of the napkin holder. Grade C+, $200 – 350.

Plate 8

Top Left: *Maker not marked, Number 0234. (Located: Meriden Silver Plate Co.)* A cat plays with a ball of yarn alongside the napkin holder. Grade D+, under $200. **Top Right:** *Maker and number not marked. (Located: James W. Tufts, Number 1594.)* A cat with back arched and tail erect stands beside a napkin holder. Grade D+, under $200. **Bottom Left:** *Meriden Silver Plate Co., Number 293.* A cat on its back, lying on a base in the shape of a square cushion, balances a napkin holder with its paws. Grade C+, $200 – 350. **Bottom Right:** *Maker and number not marked.* *(Located: James W. Tufts, Number 1596.)* A medium-sized cat stands on its hind legs alongside the napkin holder. Grade D+, under $200.

Plate 9

Maker and number not marked. A small cat sits in front of a bright-cut napkin holder. A banner-shaped space for engraving is found on top of the napkin holder. Grade D+, under $200.

Plate 10

Maker and number not marked. A nicely modeled, large, seated cat with glass eyes wears a pretty bow on the back of its neck. Grade C+, $200 – 350.

Plate 11

Maker and number not marked. (Probably Wilcox Silver Plate Co.) A seated cat with glass eyes features a napkin holder that forms the body. The holder is engraved with a bird and foliate decorations. Grade B, $350 – 500.

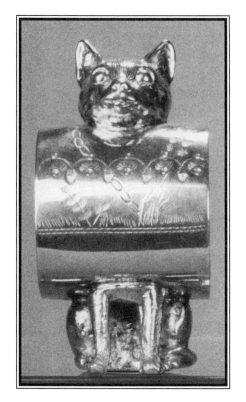

Plate 12

Maker and number not marked. (Possibly Wilcox Silver Plate Co.) A napkin holder intersects the mid-section of this seated cat, which has *no* glass eyes. Grade C, $200 – 350.

Plate 13

Maker not marked, Number 0235. (Located: Meriden Silver Plate Co.) A medium-sized cat rests its paws against a narrow, decorated napkin holder. Grade C+, $200 – 350.

Dogs

Possibly one of the largest and most favorite subjects of figural napkin ring manufacturers was the dog. A few of the pedigree breeds represented are the greyhound, poodle, dachshund, terrier, and bulldog. At the same time, mixed-breeds were very popular. Dogs are shown in various engaging poses of obedience, ferocity, and play. Because of the realistic postures exhibited by most of the animals, one cannot help but believe that the designers used their own pets and their habits as models.

A popular subject in Victorian times, as well as the present, dog figurals are collected by many as their single interest.

Plate 14

Maker and number not marked. A handsome, solid-cast dachshund carries a scalloped and decorated-edged napkin holder with engraving on top. Grade B, $350 – 500.

Plate 15

Hartford Silver Plate Co., Number 017. A dog plays a horn while seated on its hind legs. The square, ball-footed base has a carpet-like design with a fringed edge. Grade C+, $200 – 350.

Plate 16

Aurora Silver Plate Co., Number 27. A little fluffy dog stands on its hind legs to view an excited bird atop the napkin holder. This napkin ring is a small scaled object, produced for a child. Grade D+, under $200.

Plate 17

Meriden Britannia Co., Number 270. Small dogs, which are chained, look through the door openings of the dog houses on each side of the napkin holder. Grade D, under $200.

Plate 18

Maker and number not marked. A barking, fluffy dog is mounted on top of a large napkin holder with stand supports at each end of the napkin holder. Grade C, $200 – 350.

Plate 19

Maker and number not marked. A small, poodle-type dog stands with forepaws on a napkin holder with a simple monogram space. Grade D+, under $200.

Plate 20

James W. Tuffs, Number 1616. A large poodle sits on its hind legs by a napkin holder on a plain, rectangular base with cut-out corners. Grade C+, $200 – 350.

Plate 21

Derby Silver Co., Number 515. A fluffy dog holds a wishbone in its mouth. Bright-cut engraved leaves decorate the napkin holder, which is balanced by overlapping oak leaves that serve as a base. (Note: The leaves should sit flat for proper support.) Grade D+, under $200.

Plate 22

Derby Silver Co., Number 303. A small, fluffy dog with a wishbone in its mouth stands on a fancy, cast base and balances a napkin holder on its back. Grade C, $200 – 350.

Plate 24

F.B. Rogers Silver Co., Number 287. A Welsh corgi (Pembroke) wears a cord collar with ball tassels while seated beside a beaded-edged napkin holder. (Reed & Barton produced the terrier using a different style napkin holder with number 1445. Both companies were located in Taunton, Massachusetts.) Grade C, $200 – 350.

Plate 23

Maker and number not marked. (Located: James W. Tufts, Number 1595.) An angry looking dog charges over a fence while carrying the napkin holder on his back. Grade C+, $200 – 350.

Plate 25

A. Frankfield & Co., Number 3402. An angry looking dog, which charges over a fence, is mounted with the napkin holder on an irregularly shaped base. (Possibly issued by James W. Tufts for Frankfield & Co.) Grade C, $200 – 350.

Plate 26

Meriden Silver Plate Co., Number 285. A perky little dog pulls a sled decorated with a running fox. This ring was surely intended to win a child's attention. Grade C, $200 – 350.

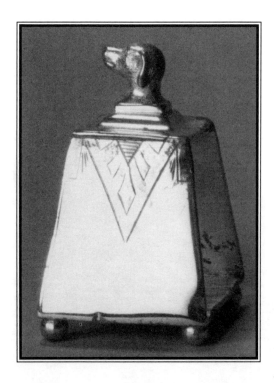

Plate 27

Maker and number not marked. A tiny, trapezoid-shaped napkin holder measures just 2¼" high from its ball feet to the top of the small dog's head. This napkin ring was intended for a wee child. Grade D, under $200.

Plate 28

Wm. Rogers Mfg. Co., Number 286. A small, begging dog sits by a flaired-and-fluted-edged napkin holder on a plain, raised rectangular base with Victorian fretwork decoration on both sides. Grade C. $200 – 350.

Plate 30

Maker and number not marked. Small dogs sit in begging positions on each side of a large, bead-and-reel-edged napkin holder. Grade D+, under $200.

Plate 29

Meriden Britannia Co., Number 336. Two small dogs stand with forepaws against the napkin holder, which is mounted on a tree-stump base. On the top of the napkin holder is a frightened bird. Grade C. $200 – 350.

Plate 31

Maker and number not marked. A large, curly haired dog stands with a heavily embossed napkin holder on its back. Grade C+, $200 – 350.

Plate 32

Top Left: *Meriden Britannia Co., Number 244.* A pug-type dog holds on its back a fancy-edged napkin holder that bears the maker's mark. Grade D+, under $200. **Top right:** *Rogers, Smith & Co., Number 364.* A small dog on its hind legs reaches for a bird on top of a fluted-edged napkin holder. (This napkin ring is also found marked Meriden Britannia Co., Canada, with the same number.) Grade D, under $200. **Bottom Left:** *Maker not marked, Number 62. (Located: Pairpoint Manufacturing Co.)* A shaggy, barking dog carries a napkin holder on its back. Grade C, $200 – 350. **Bottom right:** *Maker and number not marked.* A large, curly haired dog stands alongside a turned-edged napkin holder. Grade C+, $200 – 350.

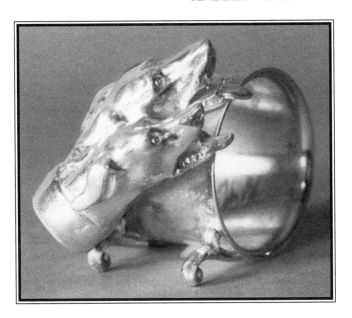

Plate 34

Maker and number not marked. A joined pair of greyhound heads are attached to a napkin holder with a turned lip edge and a pair of small scroll feet at the base on one side to maintain balance. (This napkin ring appears to be a late production. Greyhound racing is a twentieth century sport. The racing association was organized on March 6, 1926, in Miami, Florida.) Grade C, $200 –350.

Plate 33

James W. Tufts, Number 1532. A bushy tailed dog, seated on the left of a barrel-shaped napkin holder, has in its mouth the wire handle to a small bucket. The bucket is often missing. In the Tufts' catalog, the dog is illustrated seated on the right side of the napkin holder, numbered 1531; however, this napkin ring is also found marked with the number 1532. Grade C+, $200 – 350.

Plate 35

Left: *Maker not marked, Number 1185. (Located: Reed & Barton.)* Possibly the largest scaled seated dog napkin ring produced, this massive animal is an impressive 3⅞" high. A real eye-catcher and scarce form, it sold for $2.50 wholesale in 1877. Grade B+, $350 – 500. **Right:** *Maker not marked, Number 01502. (Probably Wilcox Silver Plate Co.)* A dog seated on its hind legs grips a

handle to the napkin holder with its mouth. A slightly domed base is double-tiered and footed for height and importance. (Also located marked Simpson, Hall, Miller & Co.— on a coin — number 014.) Grade C+, $200 – 350.

Plate 36

Wilcox Silver Plate Co., Number 01541. A shaggy dog is anchored at one end of an oval base decorated with a patriotic theme of stars and stripes. This base was used by Wilcox with various other figures. (Also found marked Manning, Bowman & Co. with the same number.) Grade C+, $200 – 350.

Plate 37

Simpson, Hall, Miller & Co., Number 207. A bulldog, wearing a collar fastened with a lock by a doghouse napkin holder, sits on a square base embellished with scroll feet. (This piece is also shown in an 1880s Acme Silver Co. catalog.) Grade B, $350 – 500.

Plate 38

Maker and number not marked. A small bulldog stands next to a napkin holder with appliquéd scroll borders. Grade C. $200 – 350.

Plate 39

Reed & Barton, Number 1425. A tiny, curly haired dog sits on its hind legs with its back against a narrow napkin holder, on a simple rectangular base. Grade D, under $200.

Plate 40

Maker not marked, Number 075. A small dog stands on an unusual, arched, double-leafed base in front of an unadorned napkin holder. Grade C, $200 – 350.

Plate 41

Maker and number not marked. (Located: James W. Tufts, Number 1547.) A medium-sized dog with glass eyes, a bone under its paw, sits in front of an embossed napkin holder. Grade C+, $200 – 350.

Plate 42

Wm. Rogers & Son, Number 16. A pug dog sits in a hoop on one end of a rectangular base with a leaf edge. The pedestal that supports the embossed napkin holder bolts to the base. Grade C+, $200 – 350.

Plate 43

Maker and number not marked. A small, seated pug dog with glass eyes sits with its left shoulder soldered to a slightly decorated napkin holder. Grade C, $200 – 350.

Plate 44

Webster Mfg. Co., Number 220. A small pug dog sits on a round, stepped base in front of a napkin holder supported by a foliate decorated pedestal. Grade C, $200 – 350.

Plate 46

Rockford Silver Plate Co., Number 125. A dog with its right paw up sits alongside a barrel-shaped napkin holder, elevated with scrolls. The raised rectangular base has a fluted border. Grade C+, $200 – 350.

Plate 45

Maker and number not marked. A small pug dog with glass eyes sits at attention with its back to the napkin holder. Grade C, $200 – 350.

Plate 47

Maker not marked, Number 382. A dog with glass eyes and one paw raised sits by a napkin holder with a hammered finish in the form of a tied, rolled-up scroll. Grade C+, $200 – 350.

Plate 48

Maker and number not marked. A napkin holder intersects the mid-section of this seated pug-type dog, which has no glass eyes. Grade C, $200 – 350.

Plate 49

Maker and number not marked. (Located: Wilcox Silver Plate Co., Number 4311.) A napkin holder intersects the mid-section of a pug-type dog with glass eyes. Engraved on the napkin holder is a chain which leads from the dog's neck to a post. (The engraver's sense of humor adds to the charm of this napkin ring.) Grade B, $350 – 500.

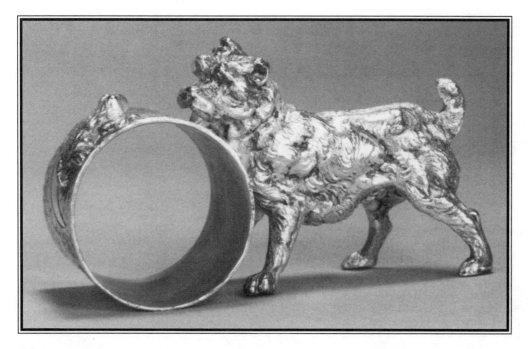

Plate 50

Maker and number not marked. (Located: Simpson, Hall, Miller & Co., Number 224.) Inspecting a small frog on top of the napkin holder is a curly haired dog. A wonderful expression of curiosity and concentration is captured on this dog's face and in its stance. Grade C, $200 – 350.

Plate 51

William Rogers Mfg. Co., Number 258. A well-sculptured hunting dog stands at attention alongside a barrel-shaped napkin holder, elevated by a short pedestal. The raised, round base adds importance. Grade C+, $200 – 350.

Plate 52

Maker not marked, Number 15. An elegant looking greyhound stands on an oval base. Its raised border is decorated with a palmette motif. The napkin holder is embellished with a floral design and a monogram plate is appliquéd on top. Grade A, $500 & up.

Plate 53

Simpson, Hall, Miller & Co., Number 014. A large seated dog grasps a handle to the napkin holder in its mouth. A round, heavy cast base is decorated with flowers in bas-relief. The maker's stamp is applied on a coin. A large piece, it stands 3⅞" high. Grade B+, $350 – 500.

Plate 54

Maker and number not marked. A small greyhound sits by a beaded-edged, hexagonal napkin holder. Grade C, $200 – 350.

Plate 55

Osborn & Co., Number 709. Two little dogs with small glass, bead-like eyes stare at a cherubic child on the napkin holder who has a tiny bird in its hands. The elevated, rectangular base has a gadroon border. Grade C+, $200 – 350.

Plate 56

Left: *Reed & Barton, Number 1485.* A very large greyhound is seated alongside the napkin holder on a raised, oval base. Grade B, $350 – 500. **Right:** *Aurora Silver Plate Co., Number 31.* A very large crouching greyhound, its paw on a ball, rests on a flat base with two chamfered corners. Grade B+, $350 – 500.

Plate 57

Simpson, Hall, Miller & Co., Number 033. A proud little dog pulls a napkin holder on wheels. (It is the same dog used to accompany Rip Van Winkle and is also found marked Meriden Britannia Co., number 033.) Grade B+, $350 – 500.

Plate 58

Left: *Simpson Hall, Miller, & Co., Number 019.* A medium-sized hunting dog crouches on a base while balancing a napkin holder on its back. Grade C+, $200 – 350. **Right:** *Wm. Rogers Mfg. Co., Number 280.* An angry looking dog with teeth bared wears a collar with a tag. He runs alongside a barrel-shaped napkin holder. Grade C, $200 – 350.

Plate 59

WMF EP I/o. A hunting-type dog stands on top of the napkin holder which rests on a pedestaled, domed base. (WMF is Wurttenbergische Metallwarenfabrik. EP represents the process of electroplating.) Grade C, $200 – 350.

Plate 60

Wm. Rogers Mfg. Co., Number is illegible. A fluffy, barking dog balances on top of the napkin holder, which rests on a base with an acanthus-leaf edge. A large horseshoe loops over the holder and dog. (Note: The napkin holder is affixed to the base with a nut and bolt, which obliterate the number.) Grade C+, $200 – 350.

Plate 61

Maker not marked, Number 243. An exceptionally tiny pug dog sits by a small napkin holder, which has a center band engraved with flowers and leaves. Grade D, under $200.

Plate 62

Simpson, Hall, Miller & Co., Number 047. Rip Van Winkle's dog is chained to a wood-grained barrel. A rectangular base with chamfered corners is decorated with a geometric design. Grade B, $350 – 500.

Combinations with Cats and Dogs

Where a cat and dog or cat and bird reside together in a household, there is always a story to tell about their relationship. Mostly bad. A few figural napkin rings confirm the torment administered by one or the other a hundred years ago. Nothing has changed.

Plate 63

Victor Silver Co., Number 542. A small bulldog seated on leaves looks up at a frightened cat atop the napkin holder. While this is a cheaply made item, they are few and far between. (Also located marked Derby Silver Co., number 542.) Grade C, $200 – 350.

Plate 64

Rogers, Smith & Co., Number 361. The heads of a bird and a cat balance a napkin holder topped with an applied cartouche providing space in its center for a monogram. This is an unusual figural. Grade C, $200 – 350.

Plate 65

Maker and number not marked. A fluffy little dog barks excitedly at a frog perched on top of the napkin holder. Grade C, $200 – 350.

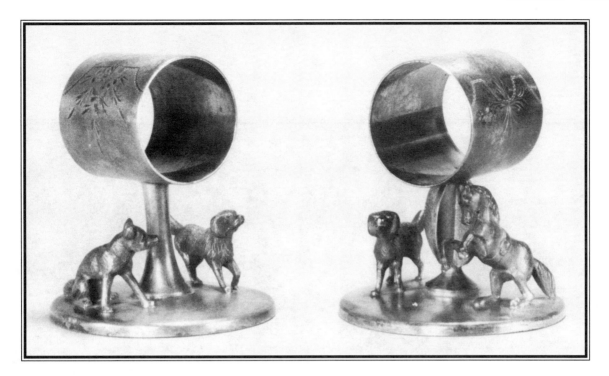

Plate 66

Left: *Webster Mfg. Co., Number 148.* A very small fox and dog on a plain, round base are placed on each side of a high pedestaled napkin holder. Grade C, $200 – 350. **Right:** *Webster Mfg. Co., Number 146.* A very small dog and horse on a plain, round base are placed on each side of a high pedestaled napkin holder. Grade C, $200 – 350.

Plate 67

Webster Mfg. Co., Number 148. A very small dog and a goat on its hind legs are mounted on a plain, round base on each side of a high pedestaled napkin holder. Grade C, $200 – 350.

Plate 68

Top Left: *F.B. Rogers Silver Co., Number 262.* A fighting cat and dog on a large, plain, round base. (See closeup next photograph.) Grade B, $350 – 500. **Top right:** *Chas. W. Hamill & Co., Number 619.* A small fluffy dog jumps toward a crouching cat, which is atop a barrel-shaped napkin holder supported by stands on a flat, rectangular base. Grade C, $200 – 350. **Bottom Left:** *Meriden Silver Plate Co., Number 275.* A barking dog, front paws on the napkin holder, attempts to reach a frightened cat on top. The raised, pressed metal, oval base has an acanthus leaf border interspersed with flowers. (This napkin ring may also be found with a variation of the base, which has a lily and lotus border design, and marked with the same maker and number. The border of the base has only a slight slant rather than a flared border shown above.) Grade C+, $200 – 350. **Bottom center:** *Chas. W. Hamill & Co., Number not marked.* A little dog barks at a cat crouched by the napkin holder on a plain, flat, rectangular base. Grade C, $200 – 350. **Bottom right:** *Reed & Barton, Number 1436.* Two very small cats face in opposite directions on either side of the napkin holder on a plain, rectangular base. Grade D+, under $200.

Plate 69

F.B. Rogers Silver Co., Number 262. A familiar theme taken from real life: a fighting cat and dog. A finely constructed figural of substantial weight, this napkin ring has a large, plain, round base, which is raised. Grade B, $350 – 500.

Plate 70

Homan Silver Plate Co., Number 131 or 136. A small, barking dog frightens a bird perched on the napkin holder elevated by a short pedestal. The plain, rectangular base is made interesting by large beading on the edge and fancy scroll feet. (The numbers on the underside are overstrikes, which leave a question concerning the correct number.) Grade C, $200 – 350.

Cows and Bulls

Figural napkin rings were items mainly used by city folks. Only a small number of milk cows and bulls are found as subjects for figurals, leading to the conclusion that they had little popularity except among people with related interests.

Plate 71

Meriden Silver Plate Co., Number 268. A small cow stands by a milk bucket-shaped napkin holder, which is placed in an offset angle. The heavy, raised round base depicts a meadow of flowers and leaves, which adds the weight necessary for balance. Grade C+, $200 – 350.

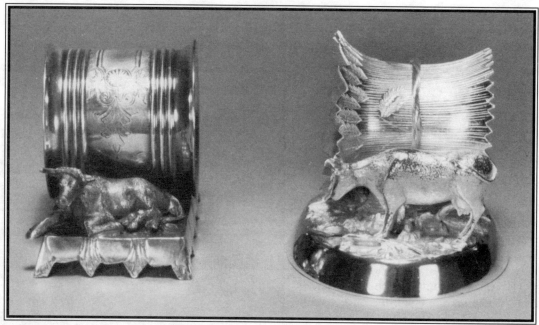

Plate 72

Left: *Maker not marked, Number 164.* A small cow lies next to a napkin holder on a rectangular base of pressed metal. Grade C+, $200 – 350. **Right:** *Wilcox Silver Plate Co., Number 01538.* A tied sheaf of wheat forms the napkin holder. In front is a milk cow standing on a raised, round base decorated as a pasture. (This attractive napkin ring is one of a few depicting country themes.) Grade C+, $200 – 350.

Plate 73

Maker and number not marked. (Located: Meriden Britannia Co., Number 243.) A small milk cow stands on an earth mound on a round base. Tree branches elevate a child-sized napkin holder. Grade C, $200 – 350.

Plate 74

Knickerbocker Silver Co., Number 1248. This small, angry looking bull stands by a decorated hexagonal-shaped napkin holder, both offset on the base. The raised, rectangular base features an embossed border design of zigzags and half rosettes. Grade C+, $200 – 350.

Plate 75

Knickerbocker Silver Co., Number 1250. A small bull stands by a bright-cut napkin holder on a fancy, raised, cast oval base. Grade C+, $200 – 350.

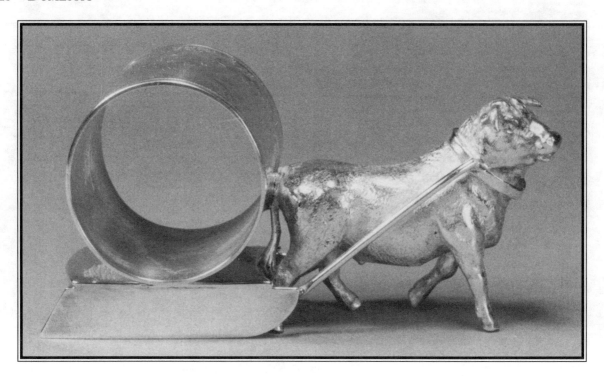

Plate 76

Middletown Plate Co., Number 84. Harnessed to a plain sled, which carries the napkin holder, a hefty bull forges ahead, an unlikely sight in real life. (Also found marked Acme Silver Co.) Grade B, $350 – 500.

Goats

Numerous different goat napkin rings were produced. While the napkin holders and bases vary from maker to maker, the castings of the goats illustrated here are identical. The old expression, "stubborn as a goat," may have swayed a buyer searching for a personality match. An interesting observation.

Plate 77

Meriden Britannia Co., Number 212. A goat pulls a beautifully chased napkin holder, mounted on wheels. Scrolls holding rosettes decorate the center section of the support to the napkin holder. Grade B+, $350 – 500.

Plate 78

Maker not marked, Number 560. This goat walks next to a bright-cut napkin holder, which is raised by a ball pedestal. Small, recessed ball feet elevate the cast round base with a scroll-edged design. Grade C, $200 – 350.

Plate 79

J. A. Babcock & Co., Number 181. A goat walks by a napkin holder on a slightly raised rectangular base featuring a zigzag and half rosettes border. (This ring is also found marked Deerpark Mfg. Co. with the same number. Knickerbocker Silver Co. produced many figural napkin rings using this identical base. Babcock & Co. was absorbed by Knickerbocker in 1894.) Grade C, $200 – 350.

Plate 80

Maker and number not marked. A goat saunters alongside a round napkin holder with a decorative design on top. Grade D+, under $200.

Plate 81

Maker and number not marked. This goat walks alongside a hexagonal-shaped napkin holder. (Located in Forbes Silver Co. catalog, number 1026, the goat is teamed with a hexagonal holder trimmed with a fine-line scroll edge. Forbes was organized in 1894 as a division of Meriden Britannia Co., but operated independently of it.) Grade D+, under $200.

Plate 82

Meriden Britannia Co., Number 195. A goat strides away from a napkin holder on a plain, rectangular, ball-footed base. Grade C, $200 – 350.

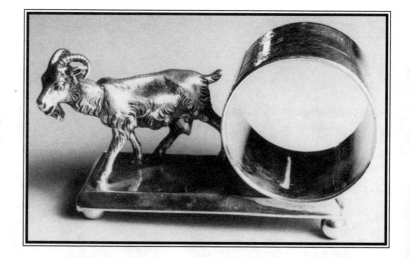

Horses and Donkeys

Before 1900, the horse provided most of the transportation in America. Although the automobile appeared in the late 1800s, paved roads were in short supply, making the horse more practical and a highly visible animal during the Victorian period. Judging from the variety of horse figural napkin rings, it seems that most known makers offered at least one horse napkin ring in their inventory. Fewer donkey napkin rings were produced.

Plate 83

Middletown Plate Co., Number 87. An unusually large, saddled horse, fastened by shafts, pulls a napkin holder on wheels. Grade A, $500 and up.

Plate 84

Meriden Britannia Co., Number 214. A small, bucking horse pulls a napkin holder on wheels. This holder is engraved with a bird inside a wreath. (This piece has also been produced with a narrow, child-sized ring, number 213. Caution: This ring has been reproduced in large numbers.) Grade C+, $200 – 350.

Plate 86

Maker and number not marked. (Probably Toronto Silver Plate Co.) A very small horse gallops on a leafy earth-mound base. The wide napkin holder is decorated with bright-cut designs. Grade D, under $200.

Plate 85

Maker and number not marked. Two small horses pull a napkin holder on a cannon-shaped cart with wheels. This is an unusual form. Grade C+, $200 – 350.

Plate 87

Derby Silver Co., Number 326. A horse's head projects from each side of a pedestaled napkin holder on a fancy, cast base. Grade C+, $200 – 350.

Plate 89

Maker and number not marked. A small, rearing horse with a child-sized napkin holder on its back is mounted with a bolt to a base of four curved, cast acanthus leaves. Grade C, $200 – 350.

Plate 88

Maker and number not marked. (Probably Henry Schade, Number 54.) A rearing horse stands on top of a napkin holder supported by a square arrangement of leaves on the base with unusual acorn-shaped feet. Grade C, $200 – 350.

Plate 90

Reed & Barton, Number 1630. This is an illustration from the 1885 Reed & Barton catalog.

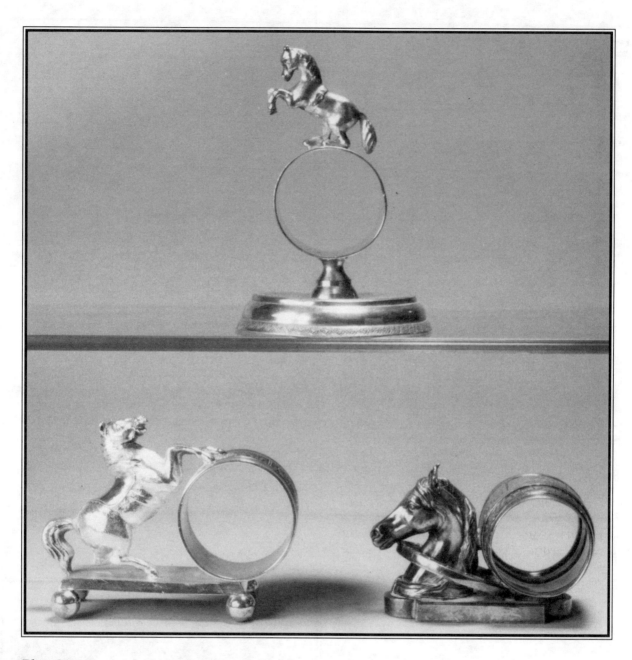

Plate 91

Top: *J. A. Babcock & Co., Number not marked.* A small horse rears on top of a napkin holder, which is elevated on a short pedestal with a raised round base. Grade C, $200 – 350. **Bottom left:** *Acme Silver Co., Number 738.* A large, saddled horse with its front hoofs on the napkin holder stands on a rectangular, ball-footed base. Grade C+, $200 – 350. **Bottom Right:** *Simpson, Hall, Miller & Co., Number 022.* A horseshoe embossed with "Good Luck" rests on a large horse's neck. The barrel-shaped napkin holder with the horse's head is mounted on a plain, raised rectangular base with half-circle extensions on the ends. Grade C+, $200 – 350.

Plate 92

Maker and number not marked. The napkin holder intersects the body of this donkey. (Was this figural produced for a stubborn or silly recipient?) Grade C, $200 – 350.

Plate 93

Maker and number not marked. A medium-sized donkey wearing a saddle stands alongside a plain napkin holder. Grade C, $200 – 350.

Plate 94

Maker and number not marked. (Located: Meriden Silver Plate Co., Number 0284.) A sleek looking horse stands in back of a rustic wood fence, both fastened to a napkin holder, which has beaded edges. Grade B+, $350 – $500.

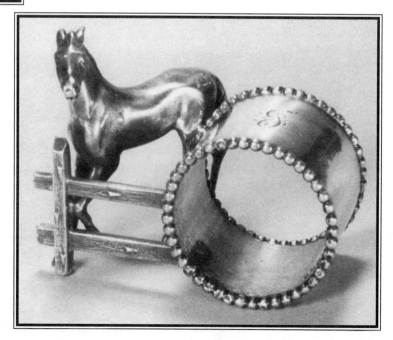

Sheep

The Victorians had a romantic interest in nature and animals, thus making a variety of animals popular subjects for figural napkin ring manufacturers. Not many sheep were made, making this category a sparse one, no doubt due to poor sales—an important business factor.

Plate 95

Barbour Silver Co., Number 13. A sheep stands on a raised, fancy rectangular base, next to the napkin holder. Grade C+, $200 – 350.

Plate 96

Meriden Silver Plate Co., Number 0279. A sheep reclines on a scroll-edged base. The napkin holder has an applied, decorative center band. Grade C+, $200 – 350.

Plate 97

Reed & Barton, Number 1505. This is an illustration from the 1885 Reed & Barton catalog.

No. 1505. Per dozen, $27.00.
Gold-lined, per dozen, 30.00.
Gold-lined and Gold Finish, per dozen, 39.00.

Plate 98

Aurora Silver Plate Co., Number 35. A sheep rests beside a short-pedestaled napkin holder on a flat base with chamfered corners. Grade C+, $200 – 350.

Bears

This is one category that did not inspire great numbers of figural napkin rings by manufacturers. The few bears on napkin rings that are known are interesting enough to stimulate conversation at a dinner table. Far from being similar, the bear figurals display originality in design.

Plate 99

Maker not marked, Number 200. A finely sculptured bear holds a rifle on its shoulder while standing on an exceptionally heavy, oval, woodland-decorated base. The napkin holder alone measures 1⅞" long, which is longer than average. Grade B+, $350 – 500.

Plate 100

Hamilton Silver Co., Number 127. A tiny bear sits on a round, raised base decorated with a scrolled edge, which matches the flared border of the napkin holder. (This ring has also been found marked Queen City Silver Co., number 3?19.) Grade C, $200 – 350.

Plate 101

Maker not marked, Number 253. A standing bear eyes a large honey bee. The base of overlapping leaves ends in a stem that wraps around the napkin holder. Grade C+, $200 – 350.

Plate 102

Left: *Maker and number not marked.* A bear seated on an oval woodland base appears to growl at a large fly on top of the napkin holder. Grade C, $200 – 350. **Right:** *Middletown Plate Co., Number 68.* A bear stands on its hind legs with front paws on the napkin holder. The rectangular base has a decorative border, which is typical of Middletown rings. Grade C, $200 – 350.

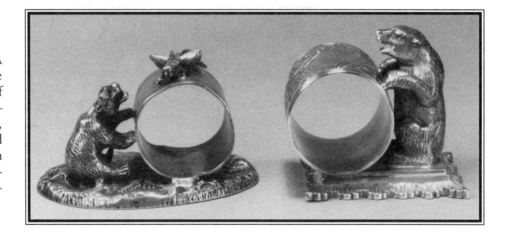

Deer

The deer figurals are among the most fragile because of their antlers, which are easily bent or broken. Often the deer with antlers missing are sold as cows or other animals. Care should be taken to examine the heads carefully when there is a possibility that the animals might be reindeer. These majestic animals represent some of the most lovely figurals when found complete and in good condition.

Plate 103

Toronto Silver Plate Co., Number 1111. A wonderful reindeer pulls a napkin holder on an ornate sled. (This napkin ring should not be confused with a reproduction of this ring described in the chapter entitled Fakes, Mistakes, and Mysteries.) Grade A, $500 & up.

Plate 104

Reed & Barton, Number 1807. A fawn wears a floral garland around its neck. The ruffled-edged napkin holder is embossed with an angel. Large, leaf-design feet support the base. Grade C+, $200 – 350.

Plate 105

Maker not marked, Number 165. A deer stands on a raised, round woodland base with a polished border. Grade C+, $200 – 350.

Plate 106

Left: *Toronto Silver Plate Co., Number 1106.* A deer stands on a raised, oval base by a napkin holder with a band of embossed flowers and an appliquéd shield suitable for a monogram. Grade C+, $200 – 350. **Right:** *Toronto Silver Plate Co., Number 1205.* A deer stands by a ruffled-edged napkin holder on a square base with a fringed, rug-type border. Grade C+, $200 – 350.

Plate 107

Meriden Britannia Co., Number 204. A handsome deer, car-rying a napkin holder on its back, stands on a plain, rectan-gular base. The napkin holder was an exclusive design of Meriden Britannia. Grade B, $350 – 500.

Plate 108

James W. Tufts, Number 1568. A small fawn lies on a shelf, which is supported by floral-topped stems with ball feet. The openwork napkin holder is unique and adds to the individuality of this piece. (This napkin ring is gold-plated, which wholesaled for $2.00 while silver plate was $1.50.) Grade C+, $200 – 350.

Plate 109

Rockford Silver Plate Co., Number 122. A well-formed stag looks backward. A flower bud is located on one side of the napkin holder. A heavy, elaborate base has double balled feet. (Note: The antlers on this deer are slightly bent.) Grade B, $350 – 500.

Plate 111

Toronto Silver Plate Co., Number 1112. An illustration from the company's 1888 catalog shows a delicate sleigh pulled by a reindeer. (Oftentimes this animal with broken antlers is incorrectly identified as a llama, doe, or "short-antlered deer." This is a good reason to carefully inspect an item for faults.)

Plate 110

Rockford Silver Plate Co., Number 196. A stag looks backward as he stands on a round base with a fluted edge. The design matches the fluting on the napkin holder. Grade B, $350 – 500.

Plate 112

Simpson, Hall, Miller & Co., Number 018. A small, nude child, that sits on top of the napkin holder, handles the reins to a reindeer. The base is a raised, rectangular shape with half-circle extensions on the ends. Grade B, $350 – 500.

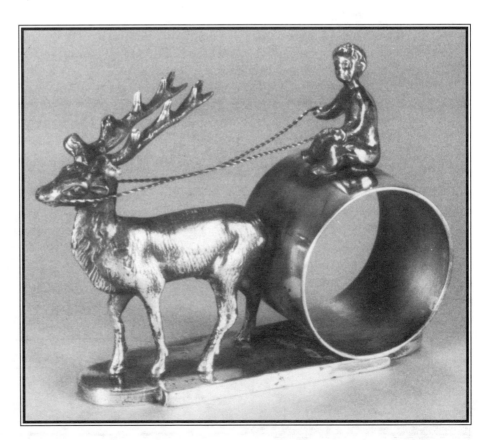

Plate 113

Webster Mfg. Co., Number 158. Two small deer lie on a mound of earth and balance the napkin holder on their backs and antlers. Grade C, $200 – 350.

Foxes and Wolves

Foxes and wolves have long been the main characters in early children's stories. Who can forget Aesop's Fables and Fairy Tales by the brothers Grimm? Foxes and wolves were seldom copied among manufacturers, thus producing an interesting variety in this category.

Plate 114

Meriden Britannia Co., Number 331. An exceptionally large fox crouches beneath the napkin holder. A branch extending along the animal's right side culminates with a leaf and bunch of grapes, which hang over the fox's head. (The ring was inspired by Aesop's fable.) Grade B+, $350 – 500.

Plate 115

Wm. Rogers Mfg. Co., Number 882. A large, plain, rectangular base with chamfered corners and curved feet holds a large, finely detailed running fox with the napkin holder alongside. A handsome and impressive piece. Grade B+, $350 – 500.

Plate 116

Left: *Homan Silver Plate Co., Number 137.* A small seated fox sits on a round, fancy, scroll-edged base with a matching pedestaled napkin holder. Grade C, $200 – 350. **Right:** *Derby Silver Co., Number 364.* A fox creeps around a bush under a napkin holder. The base is a rectangular, stepped platform. Grade C+, $200 – 350.

Plate 117

Philadelphia Plate Co., Number 01534. Two tiny foxes try to reach a bird and nest on top of the napkin holder. A scalloped, oval base rests on ball feet. (Not shown: A similar napkin ring with the same foxes on the identical base but with a bunch of grapes on the top of the napkin holder is produced by Wilcox Silver Plate Co., number 01535.) Grade C, $200 – 350.

Plate 118

Maker and number not marked. (Probably Wilcox Silver Plate Co.) A seated fox with glass eyes has a napkin holder that intersects the body. The holder is engraved with leaves and grapes. This intersecting design is one of a series employing different animals. Grade B, $350 – 500.

Plate 119

Pelton Bros. & Co., Number not marked. Little foxes with captured birds recline on each side of the napkin holder on a raised, round, decorative base. Grade C, $200 – 350.

Plate 120

Middletown Place Co., Number 69. A standing fox dressed in a coat and top hat holds a drumstick. A very small boy supports the napkin holder, which is designed as a wooden drum. Grade B, $350 – 500.

Plate 121

Barbour Silver Co., Number 9. A howling wolf is standing on a fancy, ball-footed base with a rococo scrolled edge. Grade B, $350 – 500.

Lions

The lion figural was not produced in great numbers, still it was not totally forgotten by designers. Perhaps the buyer was swayed by the noble "King of the Jungle."

Plate 122

Maker and number not marked. A lion rampant holds a beautiful, ornate, openwork napkin holder with an appliquéd monogram medallion on top. Grade C, $200 – 350.

Plate 123

Maker and number not marked. A lion rampant holds a plain napkin holder with scrollwork edges. Grade D, under $200.

Plate 124

Maker and number not marked. A very small lion reclines on a plain, rectangular base. The napkin holder, which rests on his back, provides a monogram space on top. Grade D, under $200.

Plate 125

Meriden Britannia Co., Number 153. The lion rampant—a symbol that is often representative of a country, people, or individual—stands on a plain, rectangular, ball-footed base. Grade C+, $200 – 350.

Plate 126

Toronto Silver Plate Co., Number 1104. Two diminutive lions flank the sides of the napkin holder on a raised, circular base with a polished border. The napkin holder is embossed with flowers and a monogram shield is applied on top. Grade C, $200 – 350.

Mice and Rats

No animals evoke more comments and fear than mice and rats. These animals were not pets in Victorian times but pests. Despite their unsavory reputations, these animals have a history of being the subject of Victorian tales and nursery rhymes. Remember the mouse that ran up the clock?

Plate 127

James W. Tufts, Number 1619. A mouse crouches at one end of a plain, rectangular base with cutout corners. Grade C, $200 – 350.

Plate 128

Maker and number not marked. A small rat settles down on the top of a barrel-shaped napkin holder. Crossed logs with a leaf on each side form the base. Grade D, under $200.

Plate 129

Maker and number not marked. A cute mouse climbs the side of the napkin holder, its tail serving as a stabilizer. Grade D+, under $200.

Plate 130

Maker not marked, Number 01501. (Probably Wilcox Silver Plate Co.) A long-tailed mouse nestles beside the napkin holder, which rests on a plain, round, footed base. (This napkin ring is similar to one that is marked Toronto Silver Plate Co., number 01601, but with the addition of ball feet on the base.) Grade C, $200 – 350.

Plate 131

Maker's mark is present but illegible, Number 4506. (Probably Wilcox Silver Plate Co.) A long-tailed mouse with glass eyes supports a napkin holder decorated with leaves and weeds. The body of the mouse melds into the napkin holder. Grade C+, $200 – 350.

Monkeys

The figurals of monkeys dressed as men are plays on the words "monkey around" and "grease monkey," expressions in use at the turn of the century to describe workers covered in grease, oil, and dirt who worked on machinery and as road crews. The dictionary describes the words "monkey around" as to act mischievous or in a meddlesome manner.

Monkey musical bands, similar to those depicted as napkin holders, were produced in other mediums, such as ceramics, bronze, and ivory. The monkey band figural napkin rings, shown in this section, are the only napkin rings that can be called a matching multiple set of more than two.

A word of warning: There are many monkey figurals that are being skillfully reproduced. Almost all are on bases.

Plate 132

Left: *James W. Tufts, Number 1534.* A dressed monkey holding a croquet mallet stands by a wicket napkin holder. A croquet ball, next to his foot, rests on a raised, rectangular base with chamfered corners. Grade B, $350 – 500. **Right:** *James W. Tufts, Number 1538.* The identical figure as the one on the left stands at one end of a shield-shaped base, which supports a decorated napkin holder. Grade C+, $200 – 350.

Plate 133

Maker not marked, Number 063. This seven-piece monkey band, which includes this leader, is attached to identical napkin holders of the same ornate, baroque design with gadroon borders. The monkeys' stance changes according to the instrument played, thus making this orchestra group an unusual and unique collection. (In addition to the players shown here, there are other musicians. The 1897 Sears catalog states: "We can furnish the 'Monkey Band' Napkin Ring in the following pieces, namely: The Leader, First Violin, Base [sic] Viol, Clarionet [sic], Bassoon, Triangle, Cymbals, and a few others. We have bought the entire lot of these Rings and are selling them at about one-half real value." The bass violin is illustrated with a price of 75 cents.) Grade C+, $200 – 350.

Plate 134

Maker not marked, Number 064. This monkey plays a horn (possibly a clarinet). See number 063 for general description. Grade C+, $200 – 350.

Plate 135

Maker not marked, Number 065, This monkey plays what appears to be a bass horn. See number 063 for general description. Grade C+, $200 – 350.

Plate 136

Maker not marked, Number 066. This monkey plays cymbals. See number 063 for general description. Grade C+, $200 – 350.

Plate 137

Left: *Maker not marked, Number 060.* This monkey plays a triangle. See number 063 for general description. Grade C+, $200 – 350. **Right:** *Maker not marked, Number 061.* This monkey plays the bass violin. See number 063 for general description. Grade C+, $200 – 350.

Plate 138

Maker not marked, Number 062. This monkey plays a violin. See number 063 for general description. Grade C+, $200 – 350.

Plate 139

Middletown Plate Co., Number 72. This monkey dressed in an eighteenth-century cutaway coat and a tri-cornered hat holds a cane which rests on his shoulder. The figure is sometimes found facing in a different direction on the base. In addition, the cane may be found in a downward position. Engraved on this napkin holder is the date 1884. Grade C+, $200 – 350.

Rabbits

Rabbits, both loved and hated by gardeners, were popular subjects of figural napkin rings. This grouping contains some of the most original and charming rings featuring animals. Children have loved rabbits because of the gentle rabbit characters depicted in children's books. Each manufacturer was careful to vary its designs of rabbit napkin rings, thus adding variety to this category.

Plate 140

Maker and number not marked. This magnificent, large rabbit stands on a short pedestal. At 4⅝" high, this is the largest figural ring in the rabbit category. Grade B+, $350 – 500.

Plate 141

Meriden Britannia Co., Number 233. A large rabbit sits on a plain, oval base with ball feet. Grade B, $350 – 500.

Plate 142

Maker and number not marked. A large, seated rabbit holds a napkin holder with fluted borders. This rabbit is found with napkin holders of different designs. Grade C+, $200 – 350.

Plate 143

Left: *Van Bergh Silver Plate Co., Number 67.* A large rabbit sits upright with its front legs on a decorative-edged napkin holder. Grade C+, $200 – 350. **Right:** *Southington Cutlery Co., Number 37.* The same large rabbit sits on a raised, rectangular base holding on to the napkin holder. The fluted-edged base is typical of Southington. Grade B, $350 – 500.

Plate 144

Left: *Derby Silver Co., Number 547.* This rabbit appears to be looking over the scalloped-edged napkin holder. An egg is nestled in the leaves on the other side. Grade C+, $200 – 350. **Right:** *Simpson, Hall, Miller & Co., Number 210.* A beautifully detailed rabbit crouches in front of a log napkin holder. Leaves, flowers, and berries decorate the top of the holder. Grade B+, $350 – 500.

Plate 145

Pairpoint Manufacturing Co., Number 69. A rabbit is seated by a unique, egg-shaped napkin holder with japonaiserie decorations. An original design. Grade C+, $200 – 350.

Plate 146

Derby Silver Co., Number 546. Although the chicken-on-a-wishbone napkin ring is extremely common, the rabbit by this egg-shaped napkin holder held by a wishbone is a variation not commonly seen. The napkin holder's border imitates a cracked eggshell. Grade C, $200 – 350.

Plate 147

Pairpoint Manufacturing Co., Number 68. A pair of rabbits sits on a heavily embossed, woodland base. The napkin holder is supported off the back edge of the base by a small, decorated stem. This piece is one of the prettiest and best made rings with rabbit subjects. Grade B+, $350 – 500.

Plate 148

Reed & Barton, Number 1520. A rabbit sits amid a gnarled tree limb base that supports an elevated napkin holder with fancy openwork. A dramatically different design. Grade B+, $350 – 500.

Plate 149

Victor Silver Co., Number 545. Four tiny rabbits—three of them huddled together and one standing—are positioned atop the napkin holder. Despite their diminutive size, they are finely modeled figures. A small egg rests on an oak-leaf branch which serves as a base. Grade D+, under $200.

Plate 150

Maker and number not marked. A standing rabbit and an openwork napkin holder rest on a narrow, oblong base with raised, scroll-decorated feet. Grade B+, $350 – 500.

Squirrels

Squirrels are best known for their love and need of nuts, so naturally most squirrel figural napkin rings show squirrels eating nuts. Some manufacturers varied their products by depicting the squirrels with long ears, bushy tails, or glass eyes. The squirrel was a familiar sight to visitors to parks, which was a safe and happy place for American families' picnics during the Victorian period.

Plate 151

Philadelphia Plate Co., Number 01539. A large squirrel eating a nut sits by a napkin holder on a plain, raised, oval base. (This manufacturer's number appears to be one by Wilcox, which was part of International Silver as was Philadelphia Plate Co. This squirrel also appears on a three-tiered base marked Wilcox Silver Plate Co., number 01549.) Grade C+, $200 – 350.

Plate 152

Maker and number not marked. A bushy-tailed squirrel sits on the stem of a long oak leaf, which forms the base. Two acorns are at the stem end. Scrolls trim the napkin holder's edges. Grade C, $200 – 350.

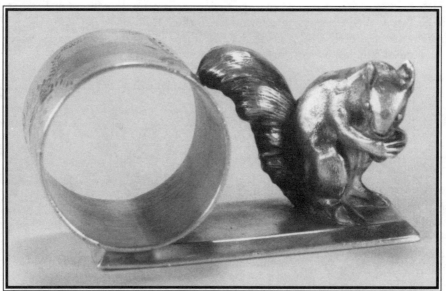

Plate 153

Rogers & Brother, Number not marked. A medium-sized squirrel with a nut sits on a plain, polished, rectangular base. Squirrels were a favorite form for use on many figural, silver-plated items. Grade C, $200 – 350.

Plate 154

Knickerbocker Silver Co., Number 7. A small squirrel stands on a raised, rectangular base with a decoratively embossed border of zigzags and half-circle rosettes. The napkin holder is elevated on balls. Grade C, $200 – 350.

Plate 155

Maker not marked, Number 42. The napkin holder intersects the body of this squirrel, which is set on a round, woodland base. Grade C+, $200 – 350.

Plate 156

Pairpoint Manufacturing Co., Number 47. A large squirrel eats a nut while seated on top of a bark-finished napkin holder balanced by leaves and nuts. (The leaves of this napkin ring are bent out of shape, placing the squirrel off balance from its correct, center position on the napkin holder.) Grade D+, under $200.

Plate 157

Reed & Barton, Number 1497. A squirrel holding a nut sits under arched oak boughs with acorns. The base is a large oak leaf. Grade C+, $200 – 350.

Plate 158

Toronto Silver Plate Co., Number 1102. A small squirrel, munching on a nut, perches on a branch amidst maple leaves. The scallop-edged holder is heavily embossed with maple leaves and holds a shield for engraving. (This piece is difficult to find without missing parts.) Grade C+, $200 – 350.

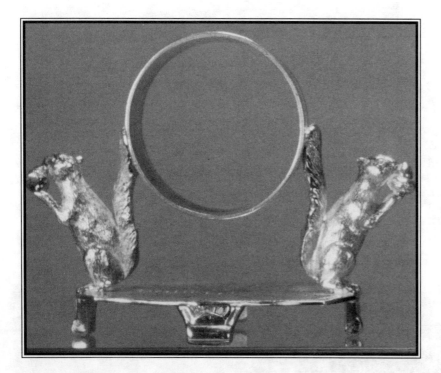

Plate 159

Bridgeport Silver Co., Number 211. Two squirrels, each eating a nut, support a napkin holder with their tails. Grade C, $200 – 350.

Plate 160

Maker and number not marked. A small, bushy-tailed squirrel, holding reins, pulls a branch with leaves and a berry, which supports the napkin holder. (The reins are sometimes missing.) Grade C, $200 – 350.

Plate 161

Maker not marked, Number 0259. (Located: Meriden Silver Plate Co.) A perky squirrel with unusually long ears sits on its hind legs by the napkin holder. Grade C, $200 – 350.

Plate 162

Van Bergh Silver Plate Co., Number 3. This large squirrel, without glass eyes, eats a nut while seated alongside a napkin holder. (This napkin ring is also illustrated as number 7 in a Barbour Silver Co. catalog.) Grade C, $200 – 350.

Plate 163

Left: *Maker not marked, Number 210.* While eating a nut, a squirrel sits on branches alongside a napkin holder. Grade D+, under $200. **Right:** *Maker and number not marked.* Small, black glass eyes distinguish this squirrel which eats a nut alongside a napkin holder. A leaf separates the squirrel from the holder. Grade C, $200 – 350.

Plate 164

Maker and number not marked. (Located: James W. Tufts, Number 1634.) A large squirrel with a bushy tail crouches under the napkin holder. Grade C, $200 – 350.

Plate 165

Simpson, Hall, Miller & Co., Number 09. As the squirrel holds a nut, it faces away from the napkin holder on a chamfered cornered, raised base. Grade C, $200 – 350.

Plate 166

Rogers, Smith & Co., Number 281. A favorite of collectors, this long-eared squirrel with glass eyes blows a horn. (This napkin ring is also found marked Meriden Britannia Co. with the same number. In 1865 Rogers, Smith & Co. was moved to Meriden, Connecticut, where it was consolidated with Meriden Britannia Co. in 1866. However, the Rogers, Smith & Co. name was continued in use.) Grade B, $350 – 500.

Plate 167

Meriden Britannia Co., Number 285. Often considered a mate to the squirrel blowing the horn, this glass-eyed squirrel holds an open song book. Grade B, $350 – 500.

Miscellaneous

During the last quarter of the nineteenth century, the circus in the United States was established as a thriving business. The Victorians, with a great curiosity regarding wild and exotic animals, flocked to see them performing in acts.

In Philadelphia a zoo was started in 1859, and after a delay was opened to the public in 1874. Newspapers and magazines printed stories of Africa and its wild animals as well as camels used for travel to the pyramids in Egypt. While the camel is generally thought of as a wild animal, it has been domesticated in the Middle East. A dining table set with wild animal napkin rings creates a striking and exotic display.

Plate 168

Maker and number not marked. A nicely modeled kangaroo and napkin holder are of fine workmanship. (This identical holder is found on American-made rings, such as Rogers & Brother and Wilcox Silver Plate Co., leading to the speculation that this ring is American despite the Australian subject.) Grade C+, $200 – 350.

Plate 169

Maker and number not marked. A napkin holder is mounted on a branch with leaves. A lizard crawls from beneath the branch to form the base. Grade C+, $200 – 350.

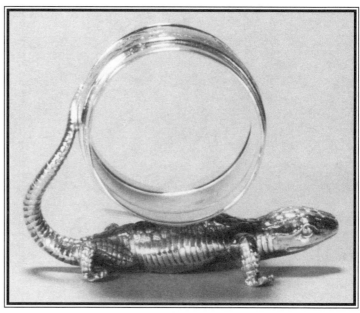

Plate 170

Southington Cutlery Co., Number 33. A lizard crawls on an earthen-like oval base, while a second lizard is draped over the top of the napkin holder. Grade C+, $200 – 350.

Plate 171

Meriden Silver Plate Co., Number 0202. A large lizard is positioned beneath the napkin holder. This lizard is found with napkin holders of different designs. (This same lizard, produced by Meriden Silver Plate, number 0201, is on a raised base with decorative legs.) Grade C, $200 – 350.

Plate 172

Knickerbocker Silver Co., Number 1249. A medium-sized elephant with a raised trunk stands by a napkin holder on a raised, oval base with a scalloped and decorative border. Grade C+, $200 – 350.

Plate 173

Maker and number not marked. An elephant with an upraised trunk stands by a cloverleaf-shaped napkin holder. Grade C, $200 – 350.

Plate 174

James W. Tufts, Number 1681. An elephant balances a plain napkin holder on its back. The stepped, rectangular base has chamfered corners. Grade B, $350 – 500.

Plate 175

James W. Tufts, Number 1567. Elephant heads form handles at each side of a pedestaled napkin holder, on an oval base covered with a geometric design. Grade C+, $200 – 350.

Plate 176

Meriden Britannia Co., Number 269. A camel on a plain, oval base with large ball feet is a nicely sculptured animal with fine detail. The camel is a domestic animal in places like Egypt and Saudi Arabia, but wild in many areas. (This napkin ring is also found marked Rogers, Smith & Co., number 269. Caution: The end of the tail is often missing.) Grade B, $350 – 500.

Plate 177

Rockford Silver Plate Co., Number 145. A giraffe stands under a palm tree. The fancy border of this big, rectangular base is supported by acorn-shaped feet. An impressive and important piece, it stands approximately 4½" high overall. (This napkin ring was produced with the giraffe placed on the left side of the napkin holder, but with the palm tree always in the center. This ring is also found marked Racine Silver Plate Co. with the same number. Racine moved in 1882 to Rockford, Illinois, and was renamed Rockford Silver Plate Co.) Grade A+, $500 and up.

Plate 178

Rogers & Brother, Number 239. Feeding on a long, leafy branch which drapes over the napkin holder, a giraffe stands on a round, woodland base with arches that extend forming the feet. (Also found marked Manhattan Silver Plate Co. with the same number.) Grade A, $500 and up.

Plate 179

Meriden Silver Plate Co., Number 309. Small boars break through fences on both sides of the napkin holder. Grade D+, under $200.

Plate 180

Wm. Rogers Mfg. Co., Number 15. An American bison stands alongside the napkin holder with a short pedestal. The rectangular base is decorated with an acanthus leaf design. Grade C+, $200 – 350.

Large, Small, Long-tailed Birds, Cockatoos and Eagles

There are hundreds of species of birds, which gave napkin-ring manufacturers a huge selection to choose from. The universal appeal of birds created a ready market for the variety of designs and for different qualities of napkin rings produced over a long period of time. Bird figurals are found in the earliest and in the latest manufacturers' catalogs, proving continual popularity of this category. Birds are by far the largest, single subject and were produced by more makers than any other figural napkin rings.

Parakeets were popular house birds during the Victorian era. Other breeds mentioned as pets in literature during that time were cockatiels, canaries, parrots, and lovebirds. Intelligent pets with distinctive personalities, many were taught to talk and perform tricks. Consequently, families loved to show off those accomplishments to visitors.

Identifying various breeds of birds is difficult without color for use as a guide. It is believed that designers took artistic license with smaller birds without keeping a particular species in mind.

In the search for identification of the various birds mounted on napkin rings, an expert on birds asked about the color. When told "silver," she replied, "Never heard of a silver bird."

Plate 181

Meriden Britannia Co., Number 230. A nicely modeled bird perches on a tangle of branches. The small Meriden mark is stamped under the bird's tail. Grade C+, $200 – 350.

Plate 182

Pairpoint Manufacturing Co., Number 8. A cockatoo perches on a ball which rests on scrolled work atop a plain, raised, circular base. Grade D+, under $200.

Plate 183

Reed & Barton, Number 1310. A long-tailed bird with spread wings perches on a small ball on top of the napkin holder. A unique structure that distinguishes this ring is a twisted rope that drapes from the ball pedestal to a small flower. It ends with a fan-like piece anchored at the ornate base. Grade C, $200 – 350.

Plate 184

E.G. Webster & Bro., Number 166. A cockatiel perches on a flower connected to the napkin holder. A stem, supporting the bird's tail, extends to the draped leaf base. Four embossed strawberries are incorporated in the design of the leaves. Grade C, $200 – 350.

Plate 185

A. C. & CO., Number not marked. This figural is Australian with the maker's mark on the inside of the napkin holder. A kookaburra bird, which is about the size of a crow and has a call resembling loud laughter, is also called a "laughing jackass." Of late production, it is electroplated on nickel-silver. Grade C, $200 – 350.

Plate 186

Simpson, Hall, Miller & Co., Number 208. A bird on each side is positioned on a branch with cherries, forming the openwork, arched sides of this napkin holder. This is a distinctly different configuration for a finely cast figural napkin ring. The matching scroll feet support a stepped, square base, adding importance to a beautiful filigree ring. Grade C, $200 – 350.

Plate 187

Pairpoint Manufacturing Co., Number 12. A cockatoo with spread wings lands on a ball atop the napkin holder. Two scrolled arms extend from the bird and lead down the back of the napkin holder ending with draped leaves in two corners. Grade C, $200 – 350.

Plate 188

Webster Mfg. Co., Number 160. A bird with a deeply forked tail hovers over a bird nest. Adding interest to this ring is the shape of the base, which is not commonly seen. Grade D+, under $200.

Plate 189

Southington Cutlery Co., Number 209. Resembling a pheasant, this long-tailed bird roosts on a stump by a napkin holder. The raised, rectangular base features a fluted border. Grade D+, under $200.

Plate 190

Maker and number not marked. A long-tailed bird with a crown and spread wings perches on a leaf base. The stem of the leaf extends upward to support the napkin holder. Grade D, under $200.

Plate 191

Derby Silver Co., Number 365. A bird spreads its wings and tail beside a napkin holder on a round, tiered base. Grade C, $200 – 350.

Plate 192

Maker and number not marked. A medallion marked "Washington, D.C." on the napkin holder indicates a napkin ring of the 1920s and 1930s, produced as a practical but inexpensive souvenir. Grade D, under $200.

Plate 193

Maker and number not marked. (Located: Derby Silver Co., Number 343.) A parakeet rests upon a curved handle supported by a scrolled foot. The napkin holder on a pair of leafy scrolls is mounted on wheels. Grade B+, $350 – 500.

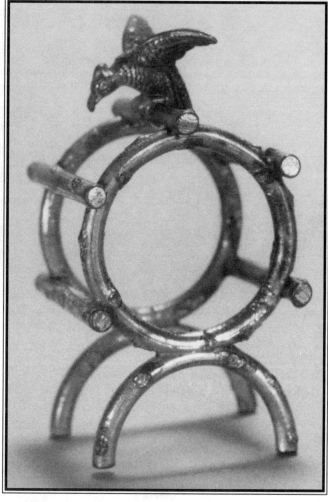

Plate 194

Maker and number not marked. Bent wood limbs form the napkin holder with a small, short-tailed bird on top. Grade D+, under $200.

Plate 195

Maker and number not marked. A plain shelf rests at the base of wooden limbs that are bent to form a holder for the napkin. A small bird, with head crest and extended wings, settles on top. Grade D+, under $200.

Plate 196

Left: *Rogers & Brother, Number 158.* A very large and beautifully cast robin stands on a branch mounted on an openwork, round base of branches and flowers. A rein around the bird's neck is attached to the napkin holder. (This piece is also found marked Meriden Britannia Co. with the same number.) Grade B, $350 – 500. **Right:** *Maker and number not marked.* A young sparrow stands next to a heavily embossed napkin holder decorated with flowers and leaves, which match the border design on the base. Grade C, $200 – 350.

Plate 197

Derby Silver Co., Number 370. A cockatoo perches on the stem of a sunflower that grows out of the circular, domed base and ends with leaves. The napkin holder is in the shape of a book. Grade C, $200 – 350.

Plate 198

Left: *Rockford Silver Plate Co., Number 146.* A fork-tailed bird alights on a scrolled stem above a garland. The round, pressed metal base resembles a cheaply constructed jar lid. While not a quality item, this piece attracts attention because of its height of 4¾". Grade C, $200 – 350. **Right:** *Rockford Silver Plate Co., Number 146.* Identical to the piece on the left, except for a different napkin holder and the size of the lid, these pieces bear the same maker's mark and number. (Note that one fork of the tail is missing the tip.) Grade C, $200 – 350.

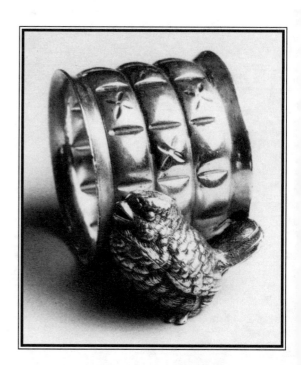

Plate 199

Meriden Britannia Co., Number 226. A baby bird perches on a tree limb that bends to form the base for a child-sized napkin holder. Grade D, under $200.

Plate 200

Maker and number not marked. (Located: Pairpoint Manufacturing Co., Number 78.) A small baby bird leans against a napkin holder decorated with a cushion design. Grade D, under $200.

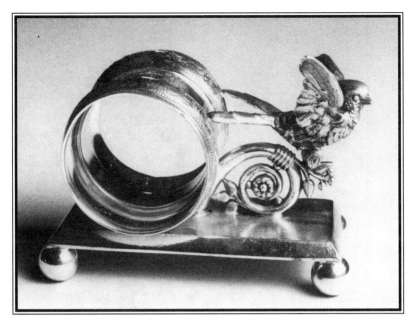

Plate 201

Meriden Britannia Co., Number 311. Preparing for flight is a small bird with a deeply forked tail. The bird is supported by a scroll on a plain, rectangular base with ball feet. Grade C, $200 – 350.

Plate 202

Maker not marked, Number 64. A small bird sits on a square napkin holder angled on a pedestal base. Grade D, under $200.

Plate 203

Rockford Silver Plate Co., Number 197. A bird with spread wings hovers over three small birds at one end of a raised, fluted, rectangular base. Vines climb up the center of the napkin holder, which repeats the design of the base. Grade C, $200 – 350.

Plate 204

James W. Tufts, Number 1668. Engraved with "Two little Birds in Blue," this napkin holder is part of a scroll on which are perched two small birds. Two ball feet are on the front for balance. Grade C, $200 – 350.

Plate 205

Rogers, Smith & Co., Number 291. A medium-sized, exotic bird with spread wings lights on a tree branch that wraps around the napkin holder from a plain, oval, ball-footed base. (This napkin holder was in popular use by Meriden Britannia, which merged with Rogers, Smith.) Grade C, $200 – 350.

Plate 206

Rogers, Smith & Co., Number illegible. A cockatoo with glass eyes sits on a C-scroll that supports the napkin holder. The square, decorative base rests on ball feet. Grade C+, $200 – 350.

Plate 207

Rockford Silver Plate Co., Number 83. Two small, open-winged birds are positioned among flowers that rise up each side of a beaded-edged napkin holder. The round base repeats the beaded border. Grade D+, under $200.

Plate 208

Maker and number not marked. (Located: Simpson, Hall, Miller & Co., Number 052.) A parakeet perches on a stem of a pair of well-detailed leaves which are placed overlapping to form a steady base. Grade C, $200 – 350.

Plate 209

Meriden Britannia Co., Number 202. A long-tailed bird rests upon the stem of a large leaf, its tips creating the feet. The banded napkin holder has in its center a leaf design with space for engraving. Grade C, $200 – 350.

Plate 210

E.G. Webster & Bro., Number 173. An open-winged bird oversees a nest of eggs and joins a napkin holder on a raised, round base. Grade C, $200 – 350.

Plate 211

Maker and number not marked. A dove with a letter held in its beak, seems ready to deliver a billet-doux (love letter). Double rings of wooden branches and leaves create a napkin holder in a unique fashion. Grade C, $200 – 350.

Plate 212

Rogers, Smith & Co., Number 229. A napkin holder is centered between a large flower and a baby bird on a branch. Grade D+, under $200.

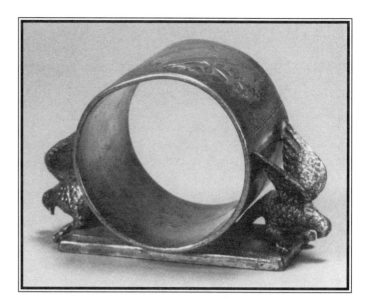

Plate 214

Meriden Britannia Co., Number 146. A matching pair of small eagles are mounted on either side of a napkin holder on a plain, rectangular base. This is possibly the most frequently found napkin ring in today's market. (This ring is also found marked Middletown Plate Co., number 74.) Grade D, under $200.

Plate 213

A. Ledig & Son, Number 311. A large sparrow stands alongside a napkin holder in the shape of a bound sheaf of wheat. Between each of the feet of the embossed, woodland base are twin arches. Grade C, $200 – 350.

Plate 215

Reed & Barton, Number 1160. A large, graceful dove holds in its beak a twisted rope that loops around, ending in a tassel. The rope forms, with the addition of a metal insert, the napkin holder. Grade C, $200 – 350.

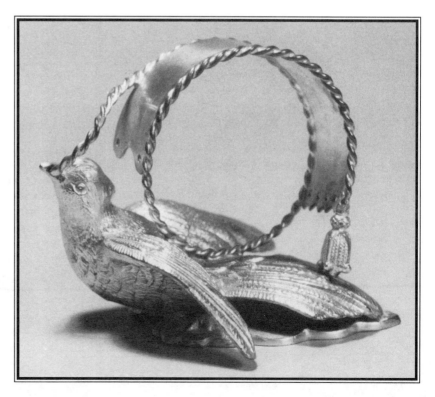

Plate 216

Left: *Manhattan Silver Plate Co., Number 240.* A very large bird stands with spread wings on an embossed, woodland base. Between the four feet are two arches on the polished border. Grade B, $350 – 500. **Right:** *Rogers, Smith & Co., Number 203.* A very large, spread-winged bird with massive claws grips a knife rest, an addition not commonly seen with figural napkin rings. This is a dual purpose table accessory. (Also found marked Meriden Britannia Co. with the same number.) Grade B, $350 – 500.

Plate 217

Reed & Barton, Number 1136. A long-tailed parrot with spreading wings sits on top of the napkin holder, which is mounted on a small base. Grade C+, $200 – 350.

Plate 218

Racine Silver Plate Co., Number 144. A large decorative scroll holds a bird on a ball and a napkin holder and rests on a plain, round, domed, pressed-metal base. Grade C, $200 – 350.

Plate 219

Left: *Maker and number not marked.* A large eagle stands on a rock with its head resting on the napkin holder. Grade C+, $200 – 350. **Right:** *Reed & Barton, Number 1517.* An eagle with long, outstretched wings grabs a wooden log, mounted on a circular, decorated base. This is a bold and impressive figural. Grade B, $350 – 500.

Plate 220

J. A. Babcock & Co., Number not marked. Two pheasants facing in opposite directions are placed on a raised, round base on each side of a pedestaled napkin holder. Grade C+, $200 – 350.

Plate 221

Wm. Rogers Mfg. Co., Number 15. A parakeet sits on an ornate scroll by a pedestaled napkin holder, mounted on a rectangular, stepped base. Grade C, $200 – 350.

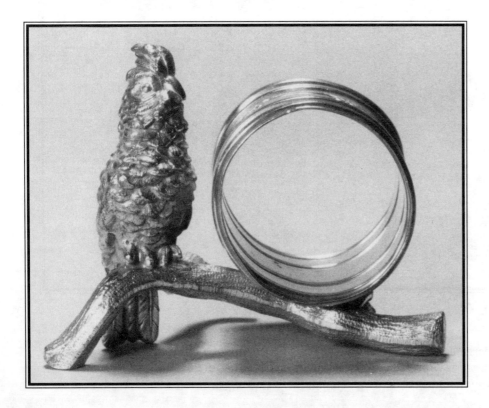

Plate 222

Maker not marked, Number 223. A beautifully formed and graceful cockatoo and napkin holder are mounted on a large curving tree branch, which forms the base. (Note: the number is found on the branch.) Grade C, $200 – 350.

Plate 223

Maker and number not marked. A parakeet rests on a rectangular napkin holder, which is positioned on a branch with a large flower and leaves. Grade C, $200 – 350.

Plate 224

Middletown Plate Co., Number 88. A pair of birds with open wings graces the sides of a decorated napkin holder, which rests on a rectangular base with an acanthus leaf border. Grade C, $200 – 350.

Plate 225

E.G. Webster & Brother, Number 167. An example of outstanding work of early master casters is this napkin ring. The parakeet sits on a flower-decorated perch, mounted on ornate, Victorian fretwork. Grade B, $350 – 500.

Plate 226

James W. Tufts, Number not marked. A cockatoo perches on a pedestal above a rectangular base with chamfered corners ending in feet. Grade C, $200 – 350.

Plate 227

Maker and number not marked. A cockatoo with glass eyes is mounted on a branch with leaves next to the napkin holder. Grade C+, $200 – 350.

Plate 228

Left: *Maker and number not marked.* A parrot with glass eyes sits on a perch atop a napkin holder supported by a sawhorse. Grade C+, $200 – 350. **Right:** *Rockford Silver Plate Co., Number 195.* A large bird with outstretched wings rests its chest against the napkin holder elevated on a short pedestal. The raised, oval base with reeded border duplicates the design on the napkin holder. Grade C+, $200 – 350.

Plate 229

Maker and number not marked. The back of this cocka-too, which has glass eyes and sits on a wooden perch, melds into the napkin holder that is engraved with flowers. Grade C+, $200 – 350.

Plate 230

Maker and number not marked. (Located: Simpson, Hall, Miller & Co., Number 026.) A cockatiel with a large flower and stem with a leaf and branch decorate the napkin holder. Grade C, $200 – 350.

Plate 231

Pairpoint Manufacturing Co., Number 9. A cockatoo with outstretched wings alights on a ball, mounted on a half-ring supported by scrollwork that also elevates the napkin holder. The base is plain, round, and raised. Grade C, $200 – 350.

Plate 232

Toronto Silver Plate Co., Number 1101. Small pheasants on each side of a highly embossed napkin holder stand on small stumps. The fancy base is composed of intertwined leaves. On the top of the napkin holder is an appliqued monogram shield. Grade C, $200 – 350.

Plate 233

Meriden Silver Plate Co., Number 263. A ring-necked pheasant struts on a raised, round base with earth formations on its upper surface. The napkin holder is supported by a branch and leaves climbing up one side. Grade C, $200 – 350.

Plate 234

Meriden Silver Plate Co., Number 246. A game bird strides alongside a napkin holder on a flat, rectangular base with chamfered corners. The holder rests on a tree stump with a branch that extends up the side. Grade C+, $200 – 350.

Plate 235

Meriden Britannia Co., Number 151. A proud peacock lends support to a napkin holder with a design that includes space for an engraved monogram or name. Grade C+, $200 – 350.

Plate 236

Meriden Silver Plate Co., Number 234. A peacock with spread wings sits atop a napkin holder on a raised, circular base. Grade C, $200 – 350.

Plate 237

Reed & Barton, Number not marked. A peacock turns his head to inspect his tail. The napkin clip is engraved "Happy New Year—Hotel St. Regis—1935." (This was most likely a party favor.) Grade C, $200 – 350.

No. 1327. Per dozen, $30.00.
          Gold-lined, per dozen,   33.00.
          Gold-lined, Gold and Oxidized, per dozen,   45.00.

Plate 238

Reed & Barton. This is an illustration from the 1885 Reed & Barton catalog.

Plate 239

Pelton Bros. & Co., Number not marked. A peacock with elaborately detailed plumage stands on a napkin holder decorated with raised bands of leaves. The elevated, domed, round base is ornamented with flowers. Grade B+, $350 – 500.

Plate 240

Meriden Silver Plate Co., Number 245. This is a classic combination of the story of the birds and bees. A large bird with wings outstretched peers around the napkin holder at a bee that supports one end of the napkin holder. The base is a flat rectangle with cutout corners. This dramatic piece is handsome. Grade B, $350 – 500.

Plate 241

Meriden Silver Plate Co., Number 271. Two pheasants decorate each side of this pretty, raised and decorative base. Their wings support the napkin holder along with a small pedestal. Grade C+, $200 – 350.

Plate 242

Pairpoint Manufacturing Co., Number 13. Two cockatoos balanced on balls support the napkin holder on their wings. The base is a flat, polished figure eight, with ball feet. Grade C+, $200 – 350.

Plate 243

Maker not marked, Number 263. (Located: Meriden Silver Plate Co.) A cut-glass napkin holder is held by a ring, topped by a small bird. This structure is held by a bolt and wing nut on a raised, elaborately embossed base. (The unit was designed to be disassembled for cleaning.) Grade C, $200 – 350.

Plate 244

Aurora Silver Plate Co., Number 17. A game bird stands by a branch and leaf alongside a spool-shaped napkin holder with a flat band in the center. The rectangular, ball-footed base has cutout corners. Grade C+, $200 – 350.

Plate 245

Meriden Britannia Co., Number 247. A bird rests upon finely cast foliage, supporting a small (1⁷⁄₁₆" diameter) napkin holder on a round, elevated, woodland base. This ring was intended for a child. (The 1886–87 Meriden Britannia Co. catalog shows more leaves rising from the floral branch.) Grade D, under $200.

Plate 246

Pairpoint Manufacturing Co., Number 70. A horseshoe base supports a highly embossed, modified triangular napkin holder with a small bird at one end of the horseshoe. Grade C, $200 – 350.

Plate 247

Left: *Rogers & Brother, Number 4?22* (the second digit may be a 3). A small bird sits by the napkin holder on an oval, ball-footed base decorated with stars and stripes. Grade C, $200 – 350. **Right:** *E.G. Webster & Son, Number 17?* (the number has an overstrike and may be 172 or 173). A cockatoo with glass eyes rests on a perch. Between the bird and the napkin holder is a rake. The base is plain and round with a polished finish. (Illustrated in the 1884 E.G. Webster & Bro. catalog is a chicken with number 172 and a bird with number 173. Most likely the correct number for this napkin ring is 173.) Grade C+, $200 – 350.

Plate 248

Maker and number not marked. A small eagle lands on a napkin holder draped with applied flowers. A cannon at the bottom provides balance and support. Grade D, under $200.

Plate 250

Henry Schade, Number 258. A split-tailed bird with spread wings perches on a ball supported by a structure composed of flowers, leaves, and berries. The top of the raised, oval base is heavily decorated. Grade C+, $200 – 350.

Plate 249

Meriden Britannia Co., Number 167. A small eagle perches on top of the napkin holder, which is elevated by a tall pedestal that rests on a domed base formed by draped petals. Grade C, $200 – 350.

Plate 251

Meriden Silver Plate Co., Number 270. An oval, scalloped base enhanced with scrolls supports a very large bird holding a stem and leaf in its mouth. The napkin holder with a decorative center band rests on both the bird's wings and head. Grade B+, $350 – 500.

Roosters, Hens, and Geese

Perhaps napkin rings with roosters and hens were selected by buyers for the relationship of the birds to some event in the life of the person for whom it was purchased. A rooster for an early riser; a hen for the cook in the family; or someone counting chickens before they hatch. There are dozens of reasons more, but the most obvious is the chicken-and-wishbone combination, which was usually accompanied by an engraved napkin holder with the message "Best Wishes" or "Good Luck." The chicken-and-wishbone figural, which was a staple in almost every silver-plate manufacturer's line, is the most commonly found. The manufacturers were hoping to put a chicken on every table.

Plate 252

Left: *Meriden Britannia Co., Number 268*. A standing hen is anchored to the napkin holder. Grade C+, $200 – 350. **Right:** *E.G. Webster & Bro., Number 172*. A chicken and garden rake are mounted on one side of a round, elevated, polished base. (This particular napkin holder is gold-lined, which when new was an added luxury at an additional cost.) Grade C, $200 – 350.

Plate 253

Meriden Britannia Co. Number 267. A hen sits by a napkin holder. (Also found with the ring attached on the opposite side, it may be marked Rogers & Bro. with the same number. Rogers & Bro. moved to Meriden, Connecticut, in 1862 and along with Meriden Britannia became a part of the formation of International Silver in 1898.) Grade C+, $200 – 350.

Plate 254

Pairpoint Manufacturing Co., Number 58. A crowing rooster stands on a rock alongside a napkin holder with a raised ring border. Grade C+, $200 – 350.

Plate 255

Osborn & Co., Number 711. Two baby chicks are situated on each side of the napkin holder, on top of which sits a small child cuddling a tiny bird. The raised, rectangular base has a gadrooned border. Grade C+, $200 – 350.

Plate 256

Wilcox Silver Plate Co., Number 01585. A baby chick stands on a rustic pallet by a unique, triangular napkin holder. Grade C, $200 – 350.

Plate 257

Wm. Rogers Mfg. Co., Number 11. A well-formed rooster stands on a tiered, oval base. The napkin holder has bright-cut engraving. (An early piece, this one was produced in the 1870s.) Grade C, $200 – 350.

Plate 258

Meriden Britannia Co., Number 181. A large, beautifully sculptured rooster stands on the handle of a farm shovel, which supports the napkin holder. The ring has a plain, rectangular base. (This is an exceptionally heavy piece that is being reproduced. Clues to the copy are new silver plating and/or missing fine details found on the originals.) Grade C+, $200 – 350.

Plate 259

Van Bergh Silver Plate Co., Number 80. A baby chick is found on each side of the napkin holder, which rests on a fancy, free-formed, scrolled base. This napkin holder has beaded edges and bright-cut engraving. Grade D+, under $200.

Plate 260

Maker and number not marked. (Located: Wilcox Silver Plate Co., Number 4304.) A chick is harnessed to a cart made up of scrolls and wheels, which carries the napkin holder. Grade B+, $350 – 500.

Plate 261

Maker and number not marked. An unusually creative design, this ring has a chick harnessed to a shaft, pulling a sled, upon which is mounted the napkin holder. The runners are embossed with a bird, leaves, and flowers on each side. Grade B+, $350 – 500.

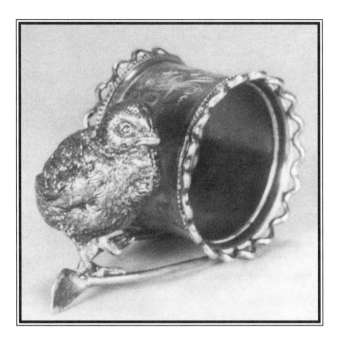

Plate 262

Maker and number not marked. A chick stands on a wishbone by a napkin holder, engraved "Best Wishes." The border is wonderfully accented with an applied, scalloped, wire edge. Grade D+, under $200.

Plate 263

Simpson, Hall, Miller & Co., Number 2361. A chick rests on a wishbone next to a beaded-edged napkin holder, engraved "Sincere Wishes." It is somewhat unusual to find the chick located to the right of the holder. Grade D+, under $200.

Plate 264

Wilcox Silver Plate Co., Number 4392. The typical chick-on-a-wishbone has the added ornaments of a footed, scroll-edged base and a large chicken foot off to the side. "Best Wishes" is engraved on the napkin holder, which has a scrolled edge that matches the round base. Grade D+, under $200.

Plate 265

Toronto Silver Plate Co., Number 799. A different placement of a chick-with-a-wishbone has the chick stepping through the wishbone. The scroll-edged napkin holder is on a short pedestal, mounted on a lobe-shaped base. Grade C, $200 – 350.

Plate 266

Left: *Meriden Britannia Co., Number 222.* A large chick stands on a plain oval base with ball feet. Grade C+, $200 – 350.
Center: *Derby Silver Co., Number 335.* See following photograph. **Right:** *Maker not marked, Number 044.* A large chick or baby bird stands on a tree branch with leaves. (These figures are difficult to classify because they have the features of both chicks and birds. This ring is possibly by Simpson, Hall, Miller based on the maker's number. It is also located in the 1888 Toronto Silver Plate Co. catalog with number 1176.) Grade C, $200 – 350.

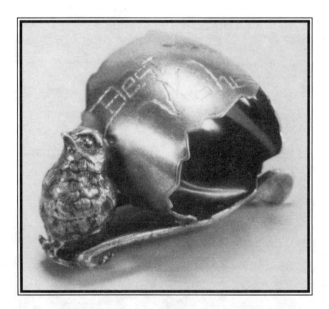

Plate 267

Derby Silver Co., Number 335. This chick with wishbone stands on a coin which bears the maker's trademark. The egg-shaped napkin holder is engraved "Best Wishes" and has cracked-shell borders. (One of the most common subjects—chick with wishbone—has been produced in one form or another over a long period of time by many companies, such as Standard Silver Co. of Toronto, Acme, and both Meriden companies.) Grade D, under $200.

Plate 268

Standard Silver Co., Ltd., Number 793. A chick with ruffled feathers stands on a branch before an upright wishbone and scroll-edged napkin holder. The holder is engraved "Sterling Wishes." Grade D+, under $200.

Plate 269

James W. Tufts, Number 1633. A chick on a chicken coop is a clever and original design. The base, resting on ball feet, has a hammered finish while the coop simulates nailed, wooden slats. Grade C+, $200 – 350.

Plate 270

Meriden Britannia Co., Number 130. A chick perches on a napkin holder with a pyramidal-shaped base with bright-cut engraving. (This chick is found on Tufts, Osborn, and Derby rings in various combinations.) Grade C, $200 – 350.

Plate 271

Derby Silver Co., Number 371. A tiny chick pops through a cracked-shell napkin holder with a small wishbone nearby. Due to its position in the photograph, the curved, fingerhold handle resting on a leaf is concealed. Grade D, under $200.

Plate 272

Derby Silver Co., Number 315. A chick sits on the manufacturer's coin with its back against the napkin holder. A simple figural, it is one of many napkin rings using this chick. Grade D, under $200.

Plate 273

Meriden Silver Plate Co., Number 0243. A goose stands on an elevated base with a geometric border. The napkin holder is embossed with floral decorations. Grade C, $200 – 350.

Cranes, Storks, Swans, and Herons

The tall crane, graceful swan, and large stork were ideal birds to decorate napkin rings. These are birds that are indigenous to specific parts of America, but are intriguing owing to their size and elegance. The stork, long ago associated with the lore of the delivery of new-born babies, could have been selected as a napkin ring for a recent mother. Swans were stocked in lakes and parks in Victorian times where children gained pleasure from feeding them and adults enjoyed watching them.

When the napkin rings with cranes, storks, and swans were first produced, these larger sized figurals commanded higher prices. For this reason, fewer were sold; therefore, fewer are currently available.

Plate 274

Simpson, Hall, Miller & Co., Number 012. A very large stork with beautiful detail stands on a raised, heavy, rectangular base with chamfered corners. The base is decorated with leaves in bas-relief. Grade B+, $350 – 500.

Plate 275

Meriden Britannia Co., Number 163. This napkin ring captures the grace of a large crane standing on one foot on a round, woodland base. Grade B+, $350 – 500.

Plate 276

Reed & Barton, Number 1126. A heron stands holding in its beak a leaf, which drapes over the top of the napkin holder. The base is raised and oval. Grade B, $350 – 500.

Plate 277

Meriden Silver Plate Co., Number 0207. A crane with out-stretched wings stands amidst tall reeds with a tiny seashell on the edge of the base. The base is oval, elevated, and highly decorative. Grade B, $350 – 500.

Plate 278

Maker and number not marked. A large, superb crane carries a stick in its beak. The napkin holder is elevated on a tree stump, which is surrounded by woodland flora on a round base. Standing 4½" tall, this is a beautifully crafted ring. Grade B+, $350 – 500.

Plate 279

Meriden Britannia Co., Number 312. A swan on a plain, oval base with ball feet is linked to the napkin holder by branches and leaves which end with a rosette. Grade C+, $200 – 350.

Plate 280

Meriden Britannia Co., Number 333. Seated on scrollwork, a cherub with wings drives a wheeled napkin holder pulled by a swan. Grade A, $500 and up.

Plate 281

Rogers, Smith & Co., Number 312. A graceful and well-modeled swan rests on an oval, ball-footed base by a napkin holder topped by two leaves. Grade C+, $200 – 350.

Plate 282

Meriden Britannia Co., Number 334. A swan with fine details pulls a napkin holder on wheels. The shaft is attached to the swan by small rings. (The napkin holder used here is a popular form employed primarily by the Meriden Britannia Co. It is often a clue to the identity of this company's unmarked rings.) Grade B+, $350 – 500.

Plate 283

Maker and number not marked. A swan with an exaggerated neck rests on elevated leaves facing an octagonal napkin holder with an applied beaded edge. The plain base has a flat, oblong shape. Grade C+, $200 – 350.

Owls

The owl—associated with sound judgment, profound wisdom, and scholarship—has been an avidly collected subject in many mediums for years. This was no secret to manufacturers who produced many owl figural napkin rings proving their clever awareness and wisdom, for these were bestsellers. A few have glass eyes.

Plate 284

Meriden Britannia Co., Number 156. A very large great horned owl is a superb rendition of this powerful bird with widely spaced ear tufts. The owl grips a branch alongside a short pedestaled napkin holder. Both are mounted on a plain, rectangular base. This is a significant piece for its size alone. Grade A, $500 and up.

Plate 286

Osborn & Co., Number 706. A large owl with glass eyes rests upon branches adjoining a napkin holder on a raised, rectangular base with a reeded border. Grade C+, $200 – 350.

Plate 285

Maker and number not marked. (Probably Wilcox Silver Plate Co.) An owl with glass eyes, the napkin holder intersecting its body, perches on a wooden stand. A quarter moon and stars decorate the napkin holder. Grade B, $350 – 500.

Plate 287

Derby Silver Co., Number 1230. An owl rests on an elevated branch and watches over oak leaves which climb up the side of the napkin holder. The rectangular base is stepped. Grade C, $200 – 350.

Plate 288

Wm. Rogers & Co., Number 257. A small owl is placed on a leaf in front of the napkin holder, which rests on a rectangular, ball-footed base. Grade C, $200 – 350.

Plate 289

Rogers, Smith & Co., Number 282. An owl standing on an open book symbolizes wisdom gained from reading. A diamond pattern with small flowers decorates the center portion of the napkin holder. (Also found marked Meriden Britannia Co. with the same number.) Grade C+, $200 – 350.

Plate 290

Rogers & Brother, Number 4394. A "long-eared" owl stands by a violin on a base designed as sheet music. The napkin holder is engraved "An Owld Friend." A chicken foot supports the napkin holder, which has an openwork, scrolled edge. Grade C+, $200 – 350.

Plate 291

Hartford Silver Plate Co., Number 028. A small owl roosts on a branch which extends from the stepped base. The napkin holder hangs from a hook fastened to the upper branch and was most likely designed for easy cleaning. Traces of gold wash remain on this ring. (This ring is also shown in the Toronto Silver Plate catalog, number 1174, priced at $2.00 each wholesale and only available in gilt.) Grade C+, $200 – 350.

Plate 292

Middletown Plate Co., Number 112. Resembling an eastern screech owl, this bird rests upon a branch with leaves in front of the napkin holder. (Also found marked Toronto Silver Plate Co., number 1152.) Grade D+, under $200.

Plate 293

Simpson, Hall, Miller & Co., Number 204. A "long-eared" owl (actually tufts of feathers) with owlets roosting on a branch is truly a beautiful ring. This square, footed base was used by this maker for many of its exceptional quality figural napkin rings. (This is shown in an Acme catalog. At one time, Acme and Simpson, Hall, Miller were operated together.) Grade A, $500 and up.

Plate 294

Maker and number not marked. A large owl with glass eyes sits on a perch alongside a beaded edged napkin holder. Grade C+, $200 – 350.

Once the novelty of figural napkin rings caught on, silver-plate manufacturers moved to make more upscale pieces to extend their lines. They wanted to profit from another fad. Bud vases with napkin holders were not only an ideal addition for sales, but a way for owners to add flowers for extra color at the table. Victorians loved the bud vases with napkin holders, judging from the number and variety produced. Most bud-vase, figural napkin rings require bases or legs for stability. A few were produced with glass-vase inserts. Those with original glass inserts still intact are the rarest. A table set with bud-vase napkin rings at each place setting never fails to evoke "oohs and ahs."

Plate 295

Left: *E.G. Webster & Bro. Number 168.* A trumpet-shaped, bud vase with morning glories climbing one side is an exceptionally well-made piece. The holder mounted on a raised, oval base is engraved with flowers. (This vase was also offered with a gold lining. A similar ring was produced by Reed & Barton, Number 1266.) Grade C, $200 – 350. **Center:** *Maker and number not marked. (Probably Taunton Silverplate Co.)* A napkin holder and trumpet-shaped, bud vase are supported with a pair of Egyptian heads and legs ending with hoof feet. Grade C, $200 – 350. **Right:** *Simpson, Hall, Miller & Co., Number not marked.* A wide arch gives firm support to the vase while forming the napkin holder. Scroll handles decorate a vase large enough for several stems of flowers. Grade C, $200 – 350.

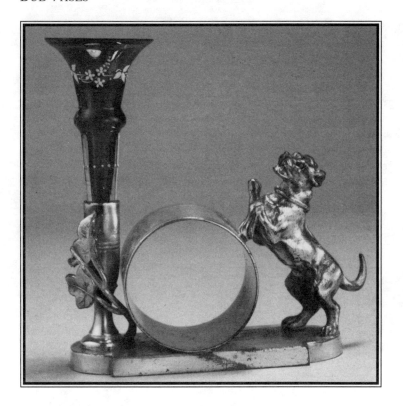

Plate 296

James W. Tufts, Number 1582. The original, enamel-decorated cranberry vase gives this piece its rarity. Three leaves drape over the vase holder. (Because the curly tail on the dog is a weak spot, it may be missing. Very expensive in the 1880s when new, this item sold for $2.75 to $3.25 wholesale depending on finish—gold or silver plate.) Grade B+, $350 – 500.

Plate 297

Maker not marked, Number 45. (Probably Taunton Silverplate Co.) A bud vase tops a napkin holder, which is supported by a stand with Egyptian heads and legs ending with hoofs. A small, detailed lion reclines on the lower shelf. (This ring, minus the bud vase, is found marked Taunton Silverplate Co., number 43.) Grade C+, $200 – 350.

Plate 298

Maker and number not marked. A pair of small, rearing horses stands with front hoofs against a pedestaled napkin holder. Atop the holder is a bulbous bud vase/toothpick container. The beautiful, openwork base is supported by ball feet. Grade B+, $350 – 500.

Plate 299

Rogers & Brother, Number not marked. A very large cherub with wings, who plays a flute, sits on a scroll with its back to a napkin holder, which supports a silver-plated bud vase. Grade A, $500 and up.

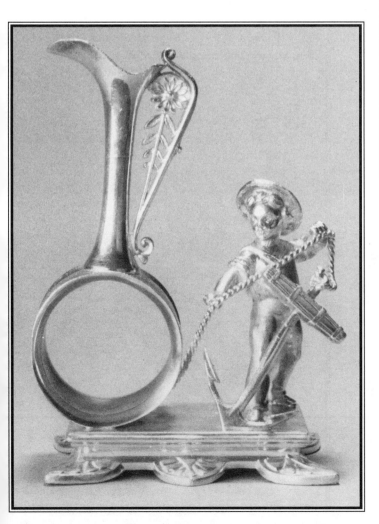

Plate 300

Reed & Barton, Number 1357. A sailor boy holds a rope that leads to an anchor. The rectangular base with six leaf-shaped feet supports the napkin holder mounted with a pitcher-shaped bud vase. (This quality piece is scarce today because of its original high cost, selling from $3.25 to $5.00 each wholesale, depending on the finish. Gold lining was extra. A bouquet of silk flowers and velvet leaves to fit the vase could be ordered at an extra cost of 50 cents.) Grade A+, $500 and up.

Plate 301

Reed & Barton, Number 1285. A large, draped cherub is seated on a pedestal with one arm resting on the napkin holder and grasps a tall, silver-plated bud vase. (The bud vase is often missing because of the fragile connection between the hand and vase.) Grade B+, $350 – 500.

Plate 302

Reed & Barton, Number 1365. A large, draped cherub is seated on a pedestal with one arm resting on the napkin holder and grasps a tall, silver-plated bud vase. The rectangular base is supported by six leaf-shaped feet. (This ring is a variation of Reed & Barton, number 1285, which is identical except for the holder and the base.) Grade B+, $350 – 500.

Plate 303

Meriden Britannia Co., Number 223. Graceful curves and a base decorated with flowers and ball feet support a black glass bud vase with enameled flowers. A small pedestal elevates the oval napkin holder. Grade B, $350 – 500.

Plate 304

Meriden Britannia Co., Number 220. A cherub with wings seated on a pedestal holds a black glass bud vase enameled with colored flowers. The raised, rectangular base is supported by flower-shaped feet. Grade B+, $350 – 500.

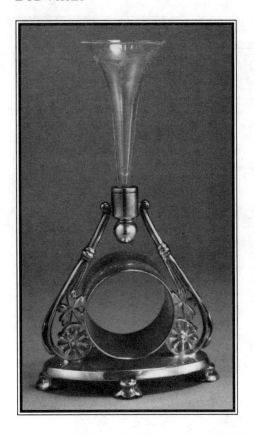

Plate 306

Rockford Silver Plate Co., Number 177. A tall fretwork handle separates a metal vase from the napkin holder. The holder and rim of the base feature geometric facets. A small bird perches at one side of the holder. Grade C, $200 – 350.

Plate 305

Meriden Britannia Co., Number 219. A pair of scrolls ending in rosettes supports a vase holder. The clear glass vase is a replacement. The original was dark, art glass. Still, a vase is a vase is a vase, because of the scarcity of all glass bud vase inserts. Grade C+, $200 – 350.

Plate 307

Aurora Silver Plate Co., Number 65. A boot is mounted on a flat, rectangular base alongside a pedestaled napkin holder. The open boot serves as a vase or tall toothpick holder. (The boot placed to the left of the napkin holder is marked Aurora, number 64.) Grade C, $200 – 350.

Plate 309

Rockford Silver Plate Co., Number 171. A fancy-footed, rectangular base holds a heavily embossed napkin holder. A butterfly and rosebud with leaves adorn the silver-plated bud vase. Grade C+, $200 – 350.

Plate 308

Acme Silver Co., Number 741. A vase with a scalloped rim is placed at one side of the napkin holder and joined to its base with a pair of leaves. A bird perches on top of the napkin holder, which is connected to the base by two flowers. Grade C, $200 – 350.

Plate 310

Pairpoint Manufacturing Co., Number 10. A very large, draped cherub with wings (3⅝" from head to toe) sits with crossed legs on a raised, two-footed base. A removable, glass bud vase mounts in a holder behind the cherub. (The vase is not the original.) Grade A, $500 and up.

Plate 311

E.G. Webster & Bro., Number 171. A gold-colored glass bud vase, which is painted in the style of Mary Gregory, shows the figure of a child. The vase is mounted in a cutout, embossed bud-vase holder. Grade B, $350 – 500.

Plate 312

E.G. Webster & Bro., Number 174. A blue-glass, bud vase is painted with the figure of a girl in the style of Mary Gregory. The vase is mounted in a cutout and embossed bud-vase holder. A scroll handle and raised napkin holder are mounted on a footed base. Grade B+, $350 – 500.

Plate 313

E.G. Webster & Bro., Number 169. A parakeet is situated on a high perch on one side of a napkin holder. On the other side is a metal, bud-vase holder with fancy openwork and embossing. The light-blue, opaque glass vase is enameled with white floral designs. The scalloped base is raised on four feet. Grade C+, $200 – 350.

Plate 314

Wilcox Silver Plate Co., Number 1899. Two small birds flank a large, silver-plated bud vase on top of a pedestaled napkin holder. Grade C, $200 – 350.

Plate 315

Hartford Silver Plate Co., Number 017. A draped, male figure runs toward a napkin holder while holding a bud vase aloft. The pink-and-white-cased glass bud vase is enameled with flowers. The square base has a rug-fringe border and rests on four ball feet. Grade B, $350 – 500.

Plate 316

Rockford Silver Plate Co., Number 199. The combination of a metal bud vase with a butterfly at its base, an elevated napkin holder and a giraffe results in a napkin ring that was probably designed to be a conversation piece. The large, scalloped base is supported on ball feet. Grade A, $500 and up.

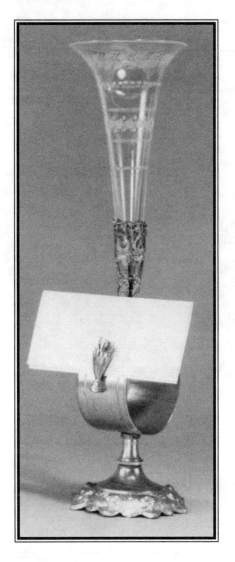

Plate 318

Maker and number not marked. A heavy metal combination bud vase and napkin holder on a large pedestal base have a stippled finish. A bird, grapes, and leaves are embossed on the object. Grade D+, under $200.

Plate 317

Maker and number not marked. The unique feature of this napkin ring is the place-card holder in the form of a hand, which is affixed to one side of the napkin holder and gives this piece its individual character. The etched- glass bud vase rests in an ornate, metal holder. Grade C+, $200 – 350.

Plate 319

Rogers, Smith & Co., Number 160. A lily leaf base raised on a rim ring supports a winged cherub, a trumpet-shaped bud vase, and a lily. The curling stem from the lily bud forms a unique prop for the napkin holder. Grade C+, $200 – 350.

Plate 320

Wm. Rogers Mfg. Co., Number 276. A kneeling, draped child balances a fluted-edged, bud vase/toothpick holder over his head. A small butterfly elevates the other side of the napkin holder. The decorative base adds interest to this ring. (Also found marked West Silver Co., number 276.) Grade C+, $200 – 350.

Plate 321

Rockford Silver Plate Co., Number 178. A draped, nude lady holds a mirror and stands by a metal bud vase and napkin holder on a raised, round base with a decorative border. Grade C+, $200 – 350.

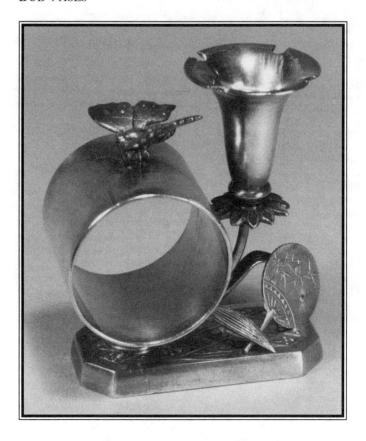

Plate 322

Simpson, Hall, Miller & Co., Number 024. This napkin ring is composed of a stylized morning glory bud vase, an Oriental fan, a butterfly, and bamboo leaves under a plain napkin holder, mounted on a rectangular base with chamfered corners. Grade C+, $200 – 350.

Plate 323

Maker and number not marked. A baby pops through a floral garland which drapes under both sides of the napkin holder to form the base. The metal bud vase is mounted on a flat band in the center of the spool-shaped napkin holder. Grade C, $200 – 350.

Plate 324

Derby Silver Co., Number 342. A small turtle supports a napkin holder on its back, alongside a metal bud vase. The stepped base is elevated on large ball feet. Grade C+, $200 – 350.

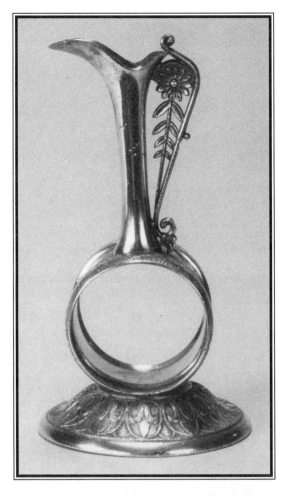

Plate 325

Reed & Barton, Number 1337. The napkin holder is mounted with a pitcher-shaped bud vase, whose scroll handle is decorated with a stylized flower, stem and leaves. The holder is atop a raised, decorated circular base. Grade C, $200 – 350.

Plate 326

Thomas Otley & Sons (Sheffield), Number not marked. Griffin-head handles placed on either side of a bud vase rest on a napkin holder with a beaded edge. The round, domed base elevates the napkin holder by a short pedestal. Grade C, $200 – 350.

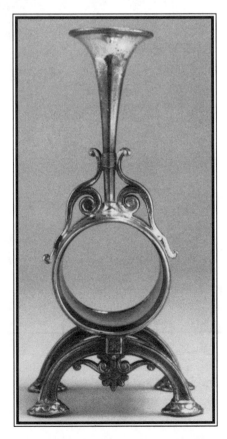

Plate 327

Maker not marked, Number 1275 marked on foot. (Located Reed & Barton.) The base composed of arches is braced at the top by a single rod from front to back. Atop the napkin holder is a trumpet-shaped, metal vase flanked by a pair of scrolls. Grade C, $200 – 350.

Victorian napkin rings in the form of chairs are interesting collectibles for their differences, yet sameness. The seat always supports the napkin holder. Judging from the styles that have so far surfaced, the rustic-, kitchen-, or outdoor-type chairs appear to have been the most popular. They also copied the styles of chairs found mainly during the last quarter of the nineteenth century. No doubt, the chair was an ideal gift for a chairperson of the board.

Plate 328

Maker and number not marked. This is a Victorian, balloon-back chair with a cushion seat. Grade D+, under $200.

Plate 329

Maker and number not marked. Bark-finished construction with a curved top rail defines this chair, which measures 4½" high. Grade D+, under $200.

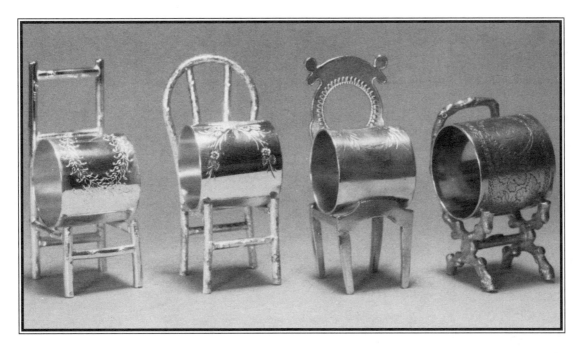

Plate 330

Left: *Maker and number not marked.* A rustic wood, ladder-back chair is 4⅜" high. Grade D+, under $200. **Left center:** *Bailey and Brainard, Number 25.* A balloon-back chair has a rustic wood finish. Grade D+, under $200 **Right Center:** *Maker and number not marked.* A Napoleon-back chair, named for the shape of Napoleon's hat, has plain legs. Grade D+, under $200. **Right:** *Maker and number not marked.* A curved-back chair, constructed of gnarled branches, copies primitive outdoor furniture of the Victorian period. Grade D, under $200.

Plate 331

Maker and number not marked. A gnarled branch chair copies an unrefined type of furniture made for use in camps and lodges. (This chair varies from the previously illustrated chair which has a lower back and different napkin holder.) Grade D, under $200.

Plate 332

Reed & Barton, Number 1585. A low stool supports a napkin holder in the form of a log with a small bird on top. Leaves with berries are embossed on one side of the holder. Grade C, $200 – 350.

Plate 333

Simons & Miller Plate Co., Number 18. A rustic wood chair with a bentwood, rounded back holds a medallion in the splat. The medallion copies the woodcarver's art of the period. Grade D+, under $200.

Plate 334

R. Strickland & Co., Number not marked. The napkin holder rests on the stretchers and front legs of a Victorian, balloon-back chair. At approximately 3¼" high, this is one of the smaller chairs. Grade D, under $200.

Plate 335

Maker and number not marked. A rustic wood chair patterned after primitive furniture with knotholes and bark finish cradles the napkin holder on the seat. Grade D+, under $200.

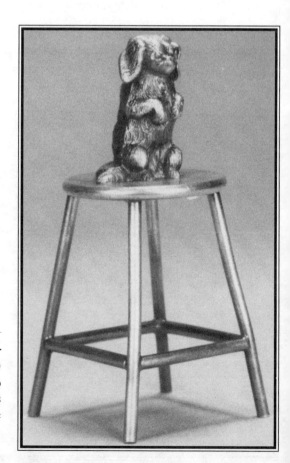

Plate 336

Maker not marked, Number 1580. (Possibly Reed & Barton.) A small dog is seated on top of a simple stool, which serves as the napkin holder. Grade C, $200 – 350.

CHARACTERS

In expanding their lines of napkin rings, the manufacturers sought the most popular subjects of the day. It was a matter of economics. For the Victorians, the most saleable were subjects that came primarily from books, the theater, mythology, and children's stories.

Rip Van Winkle, by Simpson, Hall, Miller & Co., is the only napkin ring to actually be named in a catalog. Names or words found with napkin rings in catalogs were used for identification purposes when jobbers were placing telegraphic orders. These names and words had no relation to the subject of the napkin ring.

Plate 337

Reed & Barton, Number 1492. A young girl carries a basket of provisions while standing on a low, elevated base next to the napkin holder. (To collectors of figural napkin rings, this figure is commonly called Little Red Riding Hood, although the story describes her as wearing a red cape with hood. This figure is found on other silver-plated pieces, such as card receivers.) Grade B+, $350 – 500.

Plate 338

Pelton Bros. & Co., Number not marked. This figure, identical to Reed & Barton, number 1492, stands on a higher and more elaborately decorated base and with a different napkin holder. Grade B+, $350 – 500.

Plate 339

Knickerbocker Silver Co., Number 198. A knight in shining armor holds a flaming torch and stands with a sword on a triple-tiered, round base. (Also found marked Barbour Silver Co., number 58, on a variety of bases.) Grade C, $200 – 350.

Plate 340

Maker and number not marked. (Located: Henry Schade, Number 44.) The knight in armor holding a torch and sword is an identical figure to one used by Knickerbocker. (Both Schade and Knickerbocker were New York firms.) Grade C, $200 – 350.

Plate 341

Meriden Silver Plate Co., Number 296. The satyr, a character from Greek mythology that is part beast and part man, kneels on a round, raised base and balances a napkin holder on his shoulders. (Satyrs followed Bacchus, the god of wine.) Grade C+, $200 – 350.

Plate 342

Meriden Britannia Co., Number 246. Pan, a mythological creature, which is half-human and half-goat, plays cymbals. He is seated on a ledge projecting from a triangular holder with a hammered finish. Grade C+, $200 – 350.

Plate 343

Pairpoint Manufacturing Co., Number 85. Pan, the Greek god of shepherds and hunters, dances on an oval, woodland base alongside a barrel-shaped napkin holder. Grade C+, $200 – 350.

Plate 344

Homan Silver Plate Co., Number 1500. A small clown stands with hands in his pockets. The child-sized napkin holder rests on a plain, rectangular base. (The clown was also produced with a toothpick holder.) Grade C+, $200 – 350.

Plate 345

Simpson, Hall, Miller & Co., Number 08. Rip Van Winkle and his dog stand on a hillside base decorated with ferns. A wood-grained barrel rests on Rip's shoulder. A hunting rifle and powder horn held by a chain add special interest to the figure. Because of the subject matter, impressive size (5½" high) and beautiful form, this ring is considered a rare and ultimately coveted addition to a collection. (The napkin holder may be found without wood graining. Washington Irving's short story of Rip Van Winkle was widely popular after a stage adaptation from England portrayed the hunter in 1866. Manufacturers rarely gave a name or title to a napkin ring; however, the 1887 catalog of Simpson, Hall, Miller & Co. actually titles this ring Rip Van Winkle. In the same catalog the figure is offered as decorative statuary without the napkin holder.) Grade A+, $500 and up.

No. 08.
RIP VAN WINKLE.

Silver Finish, each,	$3.00.
Silver Finish with gold lined Ring, each,	3.25.
Gold Finish, each,	3.75.
Gilt and Oxydized Finish, each,	4.50.

This can also be used as a parlor ornament by leaving off the Napkin Ring.

Plate 346

Maker and number not marked. This napkin holder is engraved "Billiken," an early 1900s character deemed to be good luck for the owner. The seated, smiling figure appeared in many mediums, including dolls and penny banks. Grade D, under $200.

Plate 347

Simpson, Hall, Miller & Co., Number 08. This is an illustration from an 1878 Simpson, Hall, Miller catalog.

Plate 348

Maker and number not marked. (Possibly Pairpoint Manufacturing Co.) A Palmer Cox Brownie holding a rifle stands by a log napkin holder as a large rabbit emerges from the side of the log. Grade B+, $350 – 500.

Plate 349

Pairpoint Manufacturing Co., Number 37. A Palmer Cox Brownie stands on a raised, round base with hands on the napkin holder. (Brownies first appeared around 1887.) Grade C+, $200 – 350.

Plate 350

Anchor Silver Plate Co., Number not marked. A Palmer Cox Brownie pushes a napkin holder. The raised, oval base is designed to resemble an earthen mound. Grade C+, $200 – 350.

Plate 352

Meriden Britannia Co., Number 165. The sphinx, an Egyptian form of a lion's body with a man's head, is an interesting Victorian subject in limited use for figural napkin rings. Grade C+, $200 – 350.

Plate 351

Meriden Britannia Co., Number 201. Triton, the mythological Greek sea god which is half man and half fish, blows a trumpet formed of a conch shell. An impressive size, this ring stands 5⅛" high. (It is sometimes referred to among napkin ring collectors as "Child of the Sea.") Grade B+, $350 – 500.

Plate 353

Meriden Britannia Co., Number 131. A winged sphinx, an intriguing figure, and napkin holder are elevated by a plain, pedestaled base. (In Greek mythology this monster with a woman's head and lion's body destroyed those unable to guess the riddles she composed.) Grade C+, $200 – 350.

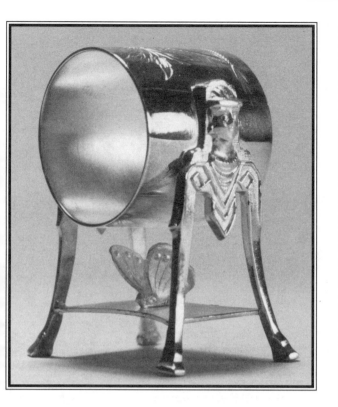

Plate 354

Aurora Silver Plate Co., Number 43. Egyptian heads on opposite sides of this napkin holder are braced with legs ending in hoofs and a shelf holding a butterfly. Grade C, $200 – 350.

Plate 355

Reed & Barton, Number 1326. Two playful elves with pointed caps balance a napkin holder on top of a fretwork pedestal. The elves are seated on blocks mounted on a heavily embossed, rectangular, raised base. Grade A, $500 and up.

Plate 356

Meriden Silver Plate Co., Number 0258. A court jester with left arm outstretched holds a staff or torch in his right hand while leaning against the napkin holder. The long, raised, oval base has an earthen surface. Grade A, $500 and up.

Plate 357

Simpson, Hall, Miller & Co., Number 016. Small, bearded gnomes carry a barrel-shaped napkin holder on poles. Grade C+, $200 – 350.

Plate 358

Reed & Barton, Number 1884. A draped female figure holds aloft a wreath. (This figure is known by several names: Miss Liberty, Columbia, Freedom, Goddess of Liberty, and Goddess of Columbia. She almost always wears a Phrygian cap, a symbol of struggles for freedom. It is unusual to find Miss Liberty with one half of the bosom exposed, especially during the Victorian period.) Grade B+, $350 – 500.

Plate 359

Homan Silver Plate Co., Number 1432. A small child dressed as a court jester stands with one hand and one foot against a pedestaled napkin holder with a beaded edge. Grade C+, $200 – 350.

COMBINATION SETS

The original purpose of combination sets was for individual use. The sets could include salt and pepper containers, butter plates (pats), and various types of condiment holders as well as a place for the napkin. Some condiment containers were of glass, even art glass. The Pairpoint Manufacturing Co. was engaged in the manufacturing of glass items and probably produced the glass salt and pepper shakers used in sets marketed by them.

One of the most difficult of all napkin ring collectibles are the combination sets because of the confusion in the identification of the separate parts. Many of these individual parts are unmarked. More often than not, the butter plates and other parts were lost or ended up on the wrong set. This problem most likely arose in the earliest days when a household possessed several sets. Taking the sets apart for cleaning, filling, or storage possibly added to the confusion. To avoid errors in reassembly of combination sets, it is a good idea to keep photographs handy of correctly assembled sets.

Combination sets were higher in cost and not as popular as the single napkin ring; however, the sets were produced in many different combinations with great variety and originality. If the proper combinations are intact, they can be quite spectacular on a dining table.

Many buyers and sellers today use the term "condiment sets," but the manufacturers' catalogs identified them as combination sets.

Plate 360

Middletown Plate Co., Number 26. Bonneted infants, which are salt and pepper shakers, rest on each side of a square napkin holder. The butter plate fits on wire hooks. The napkin holder and the base have ornate matching Victorian decorations. The infants are imitative of Kate Greenaway's drawings. Grade B+, $350 – 500.

Plate 361

Middletown Plate Co., Number 23. Copied after Kate Greenaway, an infant in long dress and bonnet sits by a square napkin holder between an open salt and a pepper shaker. A fancily designed butter plate is mounted in back. The butter plate is a square merged with a quatrefoil. Very unusual is the placement of the napkin holder under the salt cellar. Grade B+, $350 – 500.

Plate 362

Hartford Silver Plate Co., Number 656. An owl watches over a nicely fitted combination set with drop-in shakers, engraved "Salt" and "Pepper." A butter plate (possibly a replacement) nests in a plain wire rack. (Also found marked Barbour Silver Co., number 2775, and Toronto Silver Co. Number 1703.) Grade C+, $200 – 350.

Plate 363

Wilcox Silver Plate Co., Number 4100. A baby chick stands on a salt cellar in the form of a cracked egg. A matching pepper shaker sits on a napkin holder of rustic boards. A clever and charming design. Grade C+, $200 – 350.

Plate 364

James W. Tufts, Number 1459. A combination set holds a glass vinegar cruet along with a matching salt cellar and pepper shaker. A small flower and leaves decorate the top of the handle. Grade C, $200 – 350.

Plate 365

Maker and number not marked. A pepper shaker nestles in the top of this holder. Acanthus leaves on both sides of the holder form the base, making this a unique arrangement. Grade D+, under $200.

Plate 366

Wilcox Silver Plate Co., Number 1659. Tiny swan feet adorn the base of this combination set. An ornate handle and floral, scrolled attachment to the napkin holder add interest to this piece. Grade C+, $200 – 350.

Plate 367

Rockford Silver Plate Co., Number 132. This combination stand holds a glass vinegar cruet with stopper, a glass pepper shaker with metal cap, a frying-pan-shaped butter plate, and a napkin holder in the form of a log. A three-legged pot for salt is suspended from a hanger of a chimney crane that is handsomely ornamented with scrolls. Imitating a fireplace with andiron legs, this piece is novel and amusing. Grade C+ , $200 – 350.

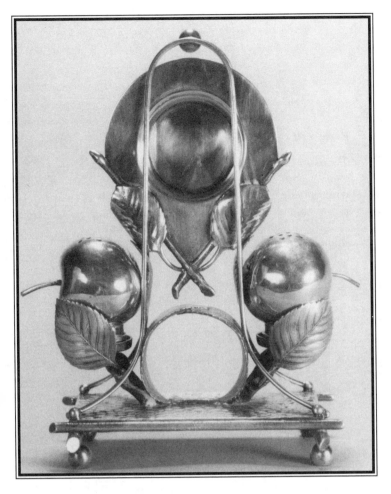

Plate 368

Hartford Silver Plate Co., Number 658. Apples with stems form the salt and pepper shakers on this unique combination set. Leaves make up the napkin holder, which rests on a rectangular base with a hammered finish. Branches and leaves are applied on the butter plate. (Also found marked Barbour Silver Co., number 2776 and Toronto Silver Plate Co. Number 1702.) Grade C+, $200 – 350.

Plate 369

E.G. Webster & Bro., Number 9. Decorated in a wonderful mix of flowers, geometric designs, scrolls, and Oriental patterns of the Victorian period, this multi-piece set is treasured for its original parts, all of which are removable including the napkin holder. Grade C+, $200 – 350.

Plate 370

Taunton Silverplate Co., Number not marked. A cherub with wings sits atop a napkin holder with a pedestal base. The napkin holder is removable as are the salt cellar and pepper shaker. All three pieces have matching, cone-shaped pedestals. (Only the base carries the maker's mark.) Grade C+, $200 – 350.

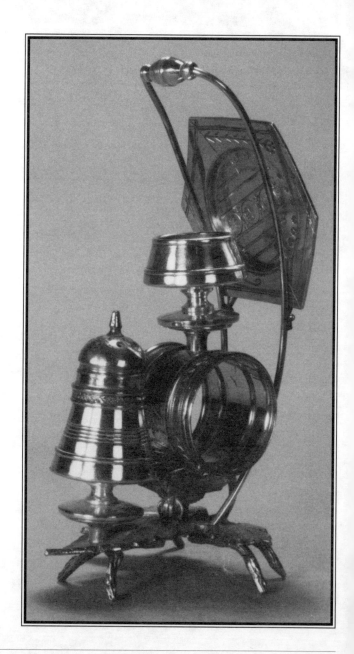

Plate 371

Meriden Britannia Co., Number 22. A large butterfly on three leaves supported by branches as legs holds the central napkin holder, on top of which rests a salt cellar. The pepper shaker completes balance for the design. A high, curved-forward handle carries the butter plate. Grade C+, $200 – 350.

Plate 372

Rogers & Brother, Number not marked. The distinctive feature on this combination set is the removable, hanging napkin holder in the form of a valise. An eye-shaped butter plate fits into a sleeve atop the round base which is elevated by four ball feet. The overhead handle is supported by two scrolled floral attachments which hold the salt cellar and pepper shaker. Grade C+, $200 – 350.

Plate 373

Pairpoint Manufacturing Co., Number 204. An Oriental fan serves as a base to this combination set. A small flower connects the fan handle to the napkin holder. The most interesting part is the butter plate, which hangs on a hook and is in the shape of a triangular, Oriental fan. The salt cellar and pepper shaker sit on pegs. Grade C+, $200 – 350.

Plate 375

Simpson, Hall, Miller & Co., Number 13. A sailor peers at a salt cellar while on his right is a wood-grained barrel napkin holder and a butter plate which serves as a sail. The dingy is elevated on a pair of stands. A super combination set! Grade B+, $350 – 500.

Plate 374

Meriden Silver Plate Co., Number 238. A draped cherub holds a salt cellar aloft. The rectangular base with cutout corners is raised on ball feet. Grade C+, $200 – 350.

Plate 376

Meriden Silver Plate Co., Number 168. A napkin holder, which is attached to the base with a bolt and nut, rests on a plain, rectangular base with four ball feet. A salt cellar in the shape of a square pan holds a perch, on which is a parrot with glass eyes. The parrot is a removable pepper shaker. Grade B, $350 – 500.

Plate 377

Rogers & Brother, Number 35. A small frog supports a leaf, which holds a removable pepper shaker owl with glass eyes. The napkin holder is attached to the stem of the leaf. Grade B, $350 – 500.

Plate 378

Maker and number not marked. (Located: Middletown Plate Co., Number 15.) A bird with outstretched wings supports a napkin holder and handle and stands between removable salt and pepper shakers. A butter plate fits on top of the round base, which is supported by four feet decorated in an anthemion design. Grade C+, $200 – 350.

Plate 379

Aurora Silver Plate Co., Number 63. A playful dog wearing a collar stands by an open salt cellar and balances a napkin holder, on which rests a butterfly. The raised, round base is decorated with a reed-and-bead border that is repeated on the napkin holder. Grade C+, $200 – 350.

Plate 380

Taunton Silverplate Co., Number 3. The napkin holder, pepper shaker, and salt cellar have matching pedestals which fit on a round base. A bird on a tall, permanently set perch serves as a handle. The zigzag border on the base is repeated on the center band of the napkin holder. Grade C+, $200 – 350.

Plate 381

Aurora Silver Plate Co., Number 5356. An Oriental man holds a long, curved, bamboo pole that provides a handle for this distinctive combination set, which includes a hanging butter plate with an Oriental design, an open salt and a pepper shaker. The round base is a mound of rocks and bamboo leaves. Grade B+, $350 – 500.

Plate 382

James W. Tufts, Number 1451. A contemplative cherub with wings stands in the center of a fancy footed base on which are mounted a butter plate, open salt, pepper shaker, and napkin holder on a small foliated pedestal. (The butter plate is a replacement.) Grade C+, $200 – 350.

Plate 383

Wilcox Silver Plate Co., Number 1655. Cupid holding a bow and quiver of arrows stands on a square base, fitted with an open salt, pepper shaker, and napkin holder. The holder is decorated on top with a small bird and nest of eggs. There seems to be a message here. Grade B, $350 – 500.

Plate 384

Simpson, Hall, Miller & Co., Number 10. A walking, draped cherub carries a silver-plated pepper shaker, which fits in a crown holder. The crown design is engraved in reverse on the pepper shaker. In front of the cherub is a salt cellar and to its back is located the napkin holder on a short pedestal. Grade C+, $200 – 350.

Plate 385

Simpson, Hall, Miller & Co., Number not marked. A pair of winged cherubs holds a curved shelf, which supports a lovely, silver-plated, crown base. Four tiny swan feet elevate the base. The pepper shaker and holder are identical to Simpson, Hall, Miller & Co, number 10. (The salt cellar, situated bottom center, is a replacement.) Grade C+, $200 – 350.

Plate 386

Southington Cutlery Co., Number 100. Two small cherubs with wings sit on opposite sides of a tall, center handle, upon which is fastened a narrow napkin holder. The square base is elevated with tassel feet. A reeded border is repeated on the base, open salt, pepper shaker, and napkin holder. Grade C+, $200 – 350.

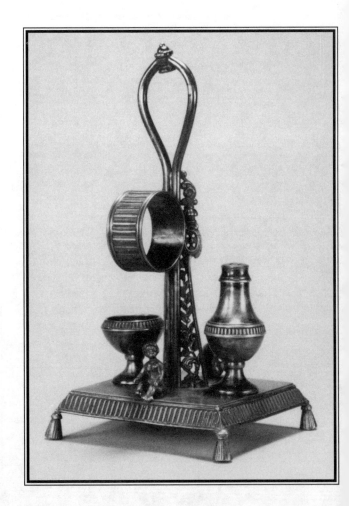

Plate 387

Left: *Taunton Silverplate Co., Number 310.* A Spanish conquistador is centered between the pepper shaker and napkin holder, which is fastened underneath the base with a wing nut. A leaf-and-berry border decorates the rectangular base with half-circle extensions. Grade C+, $200 – 350. **Right:** *Maker and number not marked.* A woman stands on the napkin holder in between an open salt and a pepper shaker, which fit into cylindrical sleeves. Six feet support a plain, rectangular base. Grade C+, $200 – 350.

Plate 388

Meriden Britannia Co., Number 16. The most interesting design features of this combination set are the rosettes that are repeated in the three scrolled feet, the handle, and the center band on the napkin holder. A bee on a ball accents the front of the napkin ring. The salt cellar and pepper shaker are anchored on pegs, mounted on the triangular base. Grade C, $200 – 350.

Plate 389

Meriden Silver Plate Co., Number 125. A draped woman stands on the end of a scroll that cradles the napkin holder and supports the salt cellar on a peg. The salt cellar and the pepper shaker, which have a matching reed design, complete this graceful arrangement. Grade B, $350 – 500.

Plate 390

Holmes & Edwards Silver Co., Number 650. An arched napkin holder separates the highly embossed salt and pepper shakers. The top of the curved wire handle is decorated with two small birds. Four feet with flower designs support the base. Grade C, $200 – 350.

Plate 391

Maker and number not marked. A curved wire handle with a bird on top extends from the base of the napkin holder to support an interestingly shaped butter plate. Salt and pepper shakers sit on pegs in front of the napkin holder. Grade C, $200 – 350.

Plate 392

Rogers, Smith & Co., Number 5. A small boy with a napkin holder overhead braces a curved handle with his hands. An open salt and pepper shaker rest on a diamond-shaped base, which is decorated on top, front, and back, with leaves. Grade C+, $200 – 350.

Plate 393

James W. Tufts, Number 1452. A ribbon band, which is highly embossed, drapes over a napkin holder with openwork design. Back-to-back flowers top the handle that supports a butter plate (a replacement). Grade C, $200 – 350.

Plate 395

R. Barrie, Number not marked. This combination set features fancy openwork at the base of the napkin holder. The salt and pepper shakers fit into narrow, embossed extensions with decorative borders. Grade C, $200 – 350.

Plate 394

Wilcox Silver Plate Co., Number 1662. An open salt and pepper shaker sit on an oval-shaped napkin holder with cutout ends. The base rests on four small swan feet. The hexagonal butter plate slips into V-shaped holders formed from rods. Grade C, $200 – 350.

Plate 396

Rockford Silver Plate Co., Number 33. A silver-plated bud vase tops the napkin holder, which is cradled in a fancy footed holder. Decorated milk-glass salt and pepper shakers are painted with landscapes. Grade C+, $200 – 350.

Plate 397

Rockford Silver Plate Co., Number 131. Racine Silver Plate Co. Two small foxes sit on either side of the base of a trapezoid-shaped napkin holder with an open salt mounted on its top. A clear glass pepper shaker and vinegar bottle nest in cupped holders. The tall handle supports the eye-shaped butter plate. (Rockford Silver Plate Co. was the name given to Racine Silver Plate Co. when it moved to Rockford, Illinois, in 1882. It is unusual to find a piece marked with both company names.) Grade C, $200 – 350.

Plate 398

Meriden Britannia Co., Number 17. An open salt and pepper shaker rest on a sweeping scroll that has a small bird and leaf in the front. A second scroll braces the napkin holder, while its upper section carries the butter plate. Grade C, $200 – 350.

Plate 399

Pairpoint Manufacturing Co., Number 225. A plethora of scrolls dominate this design. The butter plate, which is gold lined, snaps into the base and has a matching border. The block-cut glass salt and pepper shakers add a quality touch for a balanced design. Grade C, $200 – 350.

Plate 400

Wilcox Silver Plate Co., Number 1682. Rods almost form a pair of figure eights with an open salt mounted on top. The upper loop serves as the holder for the napkin, while the lower section is the resting place for the butter plate. (The maker's mark is found on the butter plate.) Grade C, $200 – 350.

Plate 401

Pairpoint Manufacturing Co., Number not marked. A pair of dolphins serves as a base for a napkin holder topped with a ring handle. The open salt and pepper shaker are balanced on a cross bar on which perches a small bird. Grade C, $200 – 350.

Plate 402

Racine Silver Plate Co., Number 112. The napkin holder is suspended within the wire handle on this set. The open salt and pepper shaker fit on pegs on the polished base. Grade C, $200 – 350.

Plate 403

Simpson, Hall, Miller & Co., Number 21. A dog on its hind legs with an open salt held in its mouth is the main attraction of this set. An openwork arch forms the handle, flanked by the napkin holder and the pepper shaker—both of which rest on scrolls. This very fancy raised base is typical of the Victorians' use of excessive design. Grade B, $350 – 500.

Plate 404

Taunton Silverplate Co. Number 2. A napkin holder rests on crossed branches. A bucket, which serves as the open salt, and a pepper shaker fit into plain, polished open holders. All three elements are composed of staves and bands, copying various forms of wooden barrels. Grade C+, $200 – 350.

Plate 405

Meriden Silver Plate Co., Number 131. The butter plate rests on the lower shelf. The upper shelf holds the pepper shaker, the napkin holder, and the open salt. A wire handle on top of the napkin holder has foliate decorations. (Also produced by Simpson, Hall, Miller & Co, number 131.) Grade C+, $200 – 350.

Plate 406

Simpson, Hall, Miller & Co., Number 7. A glass pepper shaker and vinegar cruet rest on either side of the napkin holder with an open salt on top. A bird perches on top of the handle and overlooks the butter plate. (The butter plate is a replacement.) Grade C, $200 – 350.

Plate 407

Rogers, Smith & Co., Number 14. A garland of flowers and leaves ends in a graceful scroll handle, which also supports the pepper shaker and open salt. The napkin holder is placed at one end of the plain, polished, rectangular base with ball feet. Grade C, $200 – 350.

Plate 408

Wilcox Silver Plate Co., Number 1660. Heavy looped wire forms the napkin holder, handle, and bracket for the butter plate. Four small feet in the form of swans elevate the base with a fancy border design. Grade C+, $200 – 350.

Plate 409

Maker and number not marked. An owl with glass eyes, actually a pepper shaker, sits on top of a heavily embossed, square napkin holder. The owl's head is removable for filling. Grade C+, $200 – 350.

Plate 410

Toronto Silver Plate Co., Number 1706. A reed motif is repeated throughout on the napkin holder, butter plate, salt and pepper shakers as well as the carriers, giving this combination set an integrated design. Its simplicity is really quite startling. Grade C+ $200 – 350.

Plate 411

E.G. Webster & Bro., Number 017. A strong man with a beard on bent knee balances an open salt on his head. One arm rests on the napkin holder, which is supported by an oval base with a beaded-band trim. Grade C+, $200 – 350.

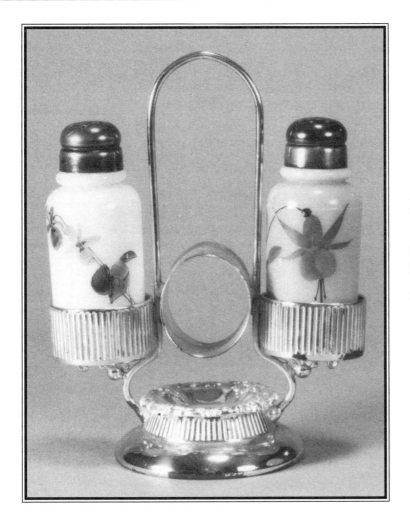

Plate 412

West Silver Co., Number 223. Decorated milk-glass salt and pepper shakers are separated by a plain napkin holder and wire handle. (The butter plate on top of the base is a replacement.) Grade C, $200 – 350.

Plate 413

Wm. Rogers Mfg. Co., Number 231. A girl, modeled after Kate Greenaway, stands with a napkin holder while riding on a stylized chariot with ornate wheels. Enamel decorated rubina glass salt and pepper shakers add elegance to this dramatic set, which is especially rare because of its original parts. A small butterfly ornaments the front end. (Rubina glass, which was first produced ca. 1885, is ruby colored glass that gradually fades to clear.) Grade A+, $500 and up.

Plate 414

Meriden Britannia Co., Number 28. A young boy pulls with reins a four-wheeled cart, which carries a napkin holder, open salt, and a pepper shaker. An elaborate scroll cradles the napkin holder. Grade A+, $500 and up.

Plate 415

Meriden Britannia Co., Number 27. A perky dog harnessed to shafts pulls a napkin holder, mounted on wheels, with an open salt and pepper shaker in tow. Scrolls surround the napkin holder. Grade B+, $350 – 500.

Plate 416

James W. Tufts, Number 1450. A cherub with large wings holds reins while seated on the napkin holder that is raised by a short pedestal. A powerful dog is harnessed to a wheeled chariot upon which are mounted an open salt, pepper shaker, and butter plate. An artfully crafted napkin ring. Grade A+, $500 and up.

Plate 417

Simpson, Hall, Miller & Co., Number 5. A combination set on wheels holds an open salt, pepper shaker, napkin holder, and butter plate. A small bird perches on the scroll handle in front. Grade B, $350 – 500.

Plate 418

Simpson, Hall, Miller & Co., Number 9. A draped cherub with wings pulls a chariot on wheels, which carries a napkin holder, open salt, pepper shaker, and butter plate—all removable. A crown with scrolls and rosettes decorates the front of the base. Grade B, $350 – 500.

Plate 419

M.W.C., Number 8305. (Possibly Meyer & Warne Co.) A peasant girl faces a napkin holder with a unique shape— a wavy square. The platform of the base has a mottled finish, which is edged by a ribbon and flower border. The salt cellar and pepper shaker fit over pegs. (This napkin holder was produced and marketed by Meriden Britannia Co. as a single holder.) Grade B+, $350 – 500.

Plate 420

Aurora Silver Plate Co., Number 352. A winged cherub sits on an undulating base that rests on three paw feet. The cherub holds a pole from the top of which hang an open salt and pepper shaker. The napkin holder is mounted on a pedestal behind the cherub with a tall handle overhead. The butter plate rests in a wire holder. Grade B+, $350 – 500.

Plate 421

Maker and number not marked. The napkin holder rests on an exquisite, ornamental, footed base. Above the napkin holder stands a bearded gnome wearing a long pointed cap. His hands touch an overhead handle. The open salt and pepper shaker fit on pegs. Grade B+, $350 – 500.

Plate 422

Wilcox Silver Plate Co., Number 4106. A napkin holder rests on a wagon parked on an earthen base. A pepper shaker in the form of a young child with a large top hat is anchored to the base by a peg. The bed of the wagon serves as an open salt when the combination napkin holder and wagon cover are removed. Grade A, $500 and up.

Plate 423

Rockford Silver Plate Co., Number 94. The principal features that make this combination set unique are the bust of the woman which decorates one end, a removable napkin holder, the ornate design of the wheels' spool-shaped spokes, and the undulating handle which ends with a leaf fingerhold. The border with its scalloped skirt displays a floral design. A wire rack supports the butter plate. Grade A+, $500 and up.

With Wings

Cupid, that timeless messenger of love with wings, has fascinated artists and writers for centuries. He was also the inspiration for a profusion of napkin rings. As the Roman god of love, some of the Cupid figures were copied from famous, old Italian paintings and sculpture. Caution: Special attention should be paid to the absence of wings where they should be present on the back of the child.

Plate 424

James W. Tufts, Number 1676. A large, draped cherub balances on one foot while clutching a vertical napkin holder with beaded edges. The polished, rectangular base has cutout corners. Grade B, $350 – 500.

Plate 425

Wilcox Silver Plate Co., Number 8206. A small cherub rests on a dome-shaped, woodland base, which also holds a narrow napkin holder, which is elevated by a ball pedestal. Grade D+, under $200.

Plate 427

Middletown Plate Co., Number 109. A tiny cherub plays with a bird amidst a branch, leaves, and an urn of flowers. The napkin holder rests on a flat base. Grade D+, under $200.

Plate 426

Aurora Silver Plate Co., Number 9. A draped cherub plays a lyre while seated on an undulating base in front of a pedestaled napkin holder. Grade C, $200 – 350.

Plate 428

Wilcox Silver Plate Co., Number 01536. Matching cherubs are seated on either side of a base with a scalloped edge and ball feet. The ends of the napkin holder are flared and formed in scallops at the edges. (Also found marked E. & H. Mfg. Co., Toronto, with the same number.) Grade C, $200 – 350.

Plate 430

Derby Silver Co., Number 320. A large oval base strewn with leaves and flowers holds an oversized cherub playing a flute while seated on a small pedestal. The napkin holder is shaped like a book, which is decorated with an Oriental fan on its cover. This is an extraordinary ring for its subject, design, and size. Grade A+, $500 and up.

Plate 429

James W. Tufts, Number 1546. Bashful Cupid holding a quiver behind his back stands by a napkin holder on a short pedestal with a plain, raised, round base. (This Cupid may be found facing in another direction.) Grade B, $350 – 500.

Plate 431

Pairpoint Manufacturing Co., Number 7. A very large, contemplative, draped cherub is seated with its back to the napkin holder. Four ball feet support a figure-eight base. The cherub, which is 4⅛" high, is bold and beautifully crafted. Grade A+, $500 and up.

Plate 432

Wilcox Silver Plate Co., Number 8255. A draped cherub captures the essence of love. With a quill pen in hand and seated on a heart-shaped napkin holder, the cherub inscribes the word "Love" on a smooth surface. Grade C, $200 – 350.

Plate 433

Left and right: *Maker and number not marked.* Pressed metal bases are fastened with bolts and nuts to the napkin holders on these napkin rings. On the left, tassels on twisted wire secure a menu card held aloft on a wire post by a cherub with wings. The cherub on the right (the wings are broken off) holds a butterfly on the back of one hand. **Left:** Grade C+, $200 – 350. **Right:** Grade D, under $200.

Plate 434

Left: *Manhattan Silver Plate Co. Number 241.* Two matching cherubs sit on a diamond-shaped base with ball feet and support a napkin holder with their wings. A third cherub decorates the top of the holder. Grade C+, $200 – 350. **Right:** *Racine Silver Plate Co., Number 149.* Small cherubs ride a seesaw atop a barrel-shaped napkin holder, supported by a small, round, earthen base. Grade C+, $200 – 350.

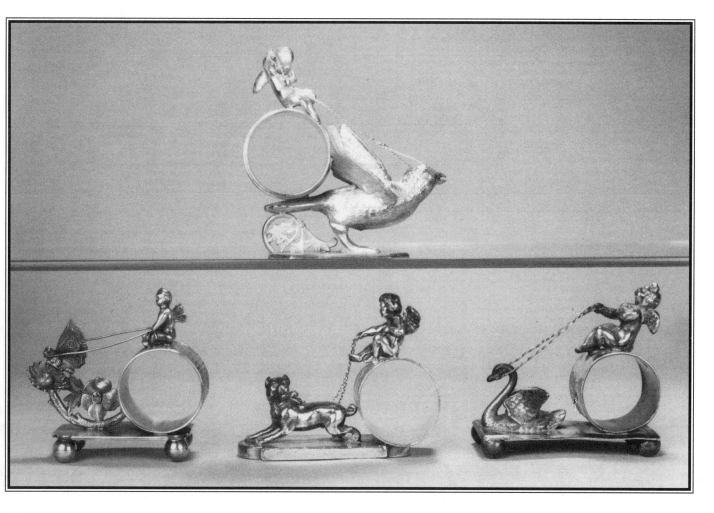

Plate 435

Top: *Racine Silver Plate Co., Number 151.* A cherub holds reins to a large bird while riding atop the napkin holder. The flat, octagonal base holds a scroll, which joins the bird's tail. (This item is also found marked Rockford Silver Plate Co., number 151.) Grade B, $350 – 500. **Bottom left:** *Rockford Silver Plate Co., Number 172.* A small cherub sits on the napkin holder while holding reins to a butterfly, which rests on a flower. The plain, rectangular base is supported by ball feet. Grade C+, $200 – 350. **Bottom center:** *James W. Tufts, Number 1543.* A cherub sits atop a napkin holder while clutching the reins to a dog. The dog wears a collar with a lock and stands on a rectangular base with half-circle ends. Grade C+, $200 – 350. **Bottom right:** *Aurora Silver Plate Co., Number 43.* A cherub sits atop a napkin holder with reins to a swan on a ball-footed, rectangular base. Grade C+, $200 – 350.

Plate 436

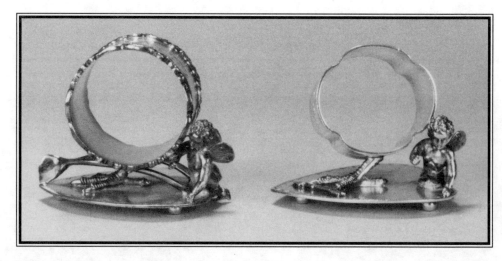

Left: *Wilcox Silver Plate Co., Number 4376.* A large, heart-shaped base holds a cherub, chicken foot, and wishbone—all the symbols necessary for the "Best Wishes" engraved on the napkin holder. (A monogram is found on the bottom of this base, which is an unusual location.) Grade C, $200 – 350. **Right:** *Wilcox Silver Plate Co., Number 4351.* A cherub kneels on a heart-shaped base supported by three ball feet. The quatrefoil napkin holder is elevated by a chicken foot with an arrow placed nearby—all for luck in love! Grade C, $200 – 350.

Plate 437

Left: *Simpson, Hall, Miller & Co., Number 051.* A cherub blows a horn while standing beside a napkin holder, which is surrounded with flowers, above a rectangular, stepped base. Grade C+, $200 – 350. **Center:** *Meriden Silver Plate Co., Number 289.* Suspended in mid-air, a cherub plays a lyre atop a napkin holder. A stem of bamboo extends from the round, dome-shaped base, embossed with leaves and flowers. (The top of the bamboo is missing some of its leaves.) Grade C+, $200 – 350. **Right:** *Rogers & Brother, Number 154.* A cherub walks while carrying a napkin holder on its back. The base is a flat rectangle. (The maker's mark is on a coin.) Grade C, $200 – 350.

Plate 438

Meriden Silver Plate Co., Number 284. A cherub pulls a sled by ropes that end in large tassels. A fox is embossed on the runners on each side of the sled, which supports the napkin holder. (This ring has been found with the sled, napkin holder, and rope placed closer to the cherub.) Grade C+, $200 – 350.

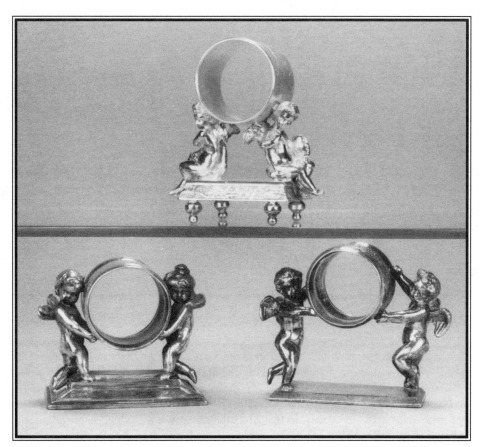

Plate 439

Top: *Hall, Elton & Co., Number 01503.* Matching, draped cherubs sit on a base with double-ball feet. One holds a painter's palette while the other has what appears to be a portrait in its hand. Grade C+, $200 – 350. **Bottom left:** *Reed & Barton, Number 1320.* Two cherubs, which differ in appearance, support a napkin holder between them on a raised, rectangular base. Grade C+, $200 – 350. **Bottom Right:** *Meriden Britannia Co., Number 200.* A pair of cherubs supports a napkin holder between them, while standing on a flat, rectangular base. (This napkin ring was re-issued as a commemorative some years ago, but is clearly marked as such on its base.) Grade C+, $200 – 350.

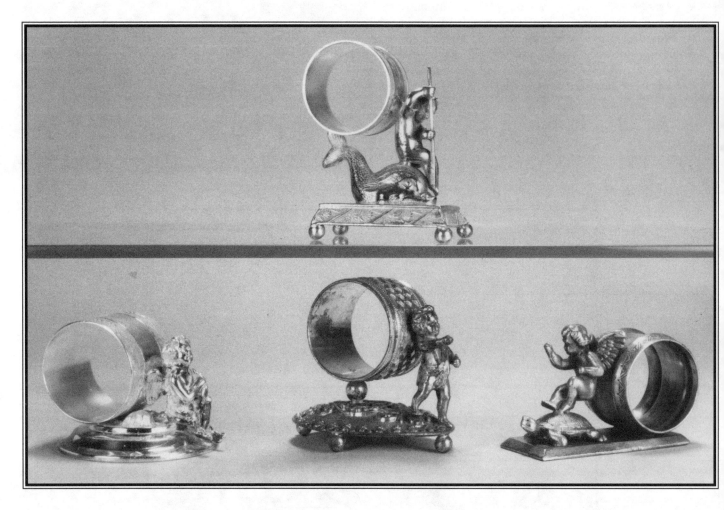

Plate 440

Top: *Maker not marked, Number 19.* A cherub holding a spear rides atop a dolphin. The napkin holder is supported by the dolphin's tail and attached to the back of the cherub. The rectangular base, elevated on ball feet, has a highly decorated border. Grade C+, $200 – 350. **Bottom left:** *Meriden Silver Plate Co., Number 219.* Seated in front of the napkin holder, a cherub with legs crossed holds an arrow and box (love gift?). Grade C, $200 – 350. **Bottom center:** *Middletown Plate Co., Number 90.* A cherub without wings and with arms extended stands in front of the napkin holder, which is raised on a ball pedestal. Grade C, $200 – 350. **Bottom right:** *Rogers & Brother, Number 82.* A cherub with one foot on a turtle leans against the napkin holder, which is on a raised, rectangular base. (Missing are reins which lead from the cherub's hand to the turtle.) Grade C, $200 – 350.

Plate 441

Reed & Barton, Number 1458. A draped cherub climbs a ladder against the napkin holder, anchored on a plain, rectangular base. This is a very small but interesting, original design. Grade C+, $200 – 350.

Plate 442

Wilcox Silver Plate Co., Number 4302. A cherub reaches for a small bird next to a pedestal under the napkin holder. The base is a rectangle with chamfered corners. Its entire upper surface is covered with an interwoven design. Grade C, $200 – 350.

Plate 443

Meriden Silver Plate Co., Number 0226. A cherub reaches for eggs in a bird's nest atop the napkin holder, which is mounted on a raised, oval base. Grade C, $200 – 350.

Plate 444

Reed & Barton, Number 1643. An illustration from the company's 1885 catalog shows a cherub pushing a narrow napkin holder.

Plate 445

Simpson, Hall, Miller & Co., Number 212. Two small cherubs with wings sit on the base. The napkin holder rests in a cradle of cross bars. Grade C, $200 – 350.

Plate 446

Maker not marked, Number 2. A partial figure of a cherub with wings decorates each side of this napkin holder. The cherub holds fabric with drapes to the sides of the holder. The base is a rectangle with half-circular extensions. Grade C, $200 – 350.

Plate 447

Maker and number not marked. A cherub with wings rests against a napkin holder with appliqued flowers and vines. Grade C, $200 – 350.

Plate 448

Wilcox Silver Plate Co., Number 01524. A unique design, this cherub with wings is seated in a stylized shell, which serves as a boat, and holds arrows that suggest oars. The open sail overhead acts as the napkin holder. Four panels, which elevate the base, are decorated with foliate designs. Grade A, $500 and up.

Plate 449

Maker and number not marked. A cherub with wings lies on a scroll-decorated rod that culminates in a shell form between wheels and provides a support for the napkin holder, which has an appliqued monogram plate. The cherub holds a floral garland with scrolls, a design that is repeated on the front end of the rod. Grade A+, $500 and up.

Without Wings

To the Victorians, sweet-faced, chubby, wingless cherubs were symbols of innocence, beauty, and love. Cherubs provided silver-plate manufacturers with a plethora of different forms, which made for variety and interest. This subject was one of the most popular for napkin rings, which endures today.

Plate 450

Reed & Barton, Number 1196. A draped cherub, seated on a tree stump, hangs onto a tasseled cord, which encircles the napkin holder. This napkin ring is 4½" high from the circular polished base to the top of the holder. (In 1887, the manufacturer offered this ring in gold plate for 50 cents extra, wholesale; however, the catalog number for silver or gold plate is 1194. This ring has been found marked with either 1194 or 1196.) Grade B+, $350 – 500.

Plate 451

Middletown Plate Co., Number 73. A nude cherub tiptoes on one foot with the other in the air as if dancing. The raised, rectangular base has an acanthus leaf border. Grade C, $200 – 350.

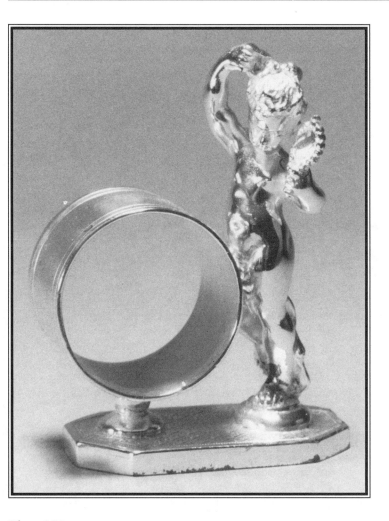

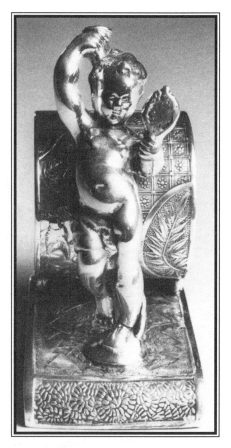

Plate 452

Wilcox Silver Plate Co., Number 4309. A draped, cherubic girl holds a mirror while primping her hair. The rectangular base with chamfered corners is decorated with a lattice design—a network of bands that cross each other at right angles. (This figure is also found on a raised, plain base with sloping ends, marked Rockford Silver Plate Co., number 101.) Grade C+, $200 – 350.

Plate 453

Rockford Silver Plate Co., Number not marked. A draped, cherubic girl holds a mirror while primping her hair. The entire base and napkin holder are embossed with a profusion of birds, flowers, and geometric patterns. Grade C+, $200 – 350.

Plate 454

Van Bergh Silver Plate Co., Number 90. A draped cherub with grapes in one hand leans against the napkin holder with a beaded edge. The cherub stands on a small, leafy base that is irregular in shape and has open spaces. Grade C, $200 – 350.

Plate 455

Left: *Maker not marked, Number 020. (Located: Simpson, Hall, Miller & Co.)* A draped cherub wearing a cap with a feather sits atop a barrel-shaped napkin holder while grasping reins to a large bird. Two ball feet support the holder. Grade B, $350 – 500. **Center:** *Maker not marked, Number 021. (Located: Simpson, Hall, Miller & Co.)* A draped cherub wearing a cap with a feather sits atop a napkin holder and grasps the reins to a butterfly resting on a flower. A pair of leaves and two ball feet form the base. Grade B, $350 – 500. **Right:** *Pairpoint Manufacturing Co., Number 52.* A draped cherub wearing a cap with a feather leans against the napkin holder. (This figure is found on pieces produced by several other companies.) Grade D+, under $200.

Plate 456

James W. Tufts, Number 1548. Can this be baby Hercules, the mythical Greek hero who was fabled for his great strength? The strain is obvious in his bulging muscles and facial expression as he pushes against a decorated, square napkin holder, embossed with circular indentations. Grade C+, $200 – 350.

Plate 457

Maker and number not marked. A large cherub with his hand to his cheek as if calling out stands with the right hand resting against a napkin holder, heavily embossed with scrolls. Grade C+, $200 – 350.

Plate 458

Meriden Silver Plate Co., Number 224. The napkin holder intersects the body of a kneeling cherub with raised arms. An odd and disproportionate form. Grade C, $200 – 350.

Plate 459

Meriden Silver Plate Co., Number 223. The bust of a cherub emerges from a field of flowers on a raised, round base, while supporting the napkin holder overhead. Grade C, $200 – 350.

Plate 460

Meriden Silver Plate Co., Number 232. A kneeling cherub with a raised drumstick prepares to strike a drum-shaped napkin holder. Open sheet music lies on the plain, round, raised base. Grade C+, $200 – 350.

Plate 461

Top: *Rogers, Smith & Co., Number 333.* A tiny cherub sits on a scroll at the base of a square napkin holder. A rosette and leaves decorate the top of the napkin holder. Grade D+, under $200. **Bottom left:** *Middletown Plate Co., Number 113.* A draped cherub artist with paint brush and palette stands on leaves while working on the napkin holder. Grade C, $200 – 350. **Botttom right:** *Middletown Plate Co., Number 92.* A small cherub holding reins rides a swan in front of a pedestaled napkin holder on a flat base. Grade C+, $200 – 350.

Plate 462

Meriden Silver Plate Co., Number 4650. A hexagonal napkin holder with a scroll border rests on a floral base. A pair of small cherubs is suspended amidst leafy scrolls on both sides of the napkin holder. Grade D+, under $200.

Plate 463

Wilcox Silver Plate Co., Number 01537. A draped cherub, wine glass in hand, sits on grape leaves atop the napkin holder. A large bunch of grapes cascade down one side, touching a fancy, raised, rectangular base. Grade B, $350 – 500.

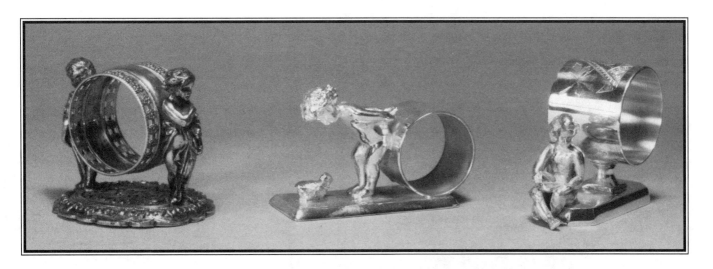

Plate 464

Left: *Toronto Silver Plate Co., Number 273.* Draped cherubs support on their backs a napkin holder with filigree borders. The fancy, slightly oval base has a scalloped edge. (Also found marked Meriden Silver Plate Co. with the same number.) Grade C, $200 – 350. **Center:** *Meriden Britannia Co., Number not marked.* A naked cherub peers at a baby bird. This is a small napkin ring intended for a young child. Grade C, $200 – 350. **Right:** *Simpson, Hall, Miller & Co., Number 02.* A draped cherub reading a book sits on the edge of the base. The napkin holder is elevated by a short pedestal. Grade C, $200 – 350.

Plate 466

Middletown Plate Co., Number 71. A cherubic boy playing soldier wears a newspaper hat and holds a sword as he rides a turtle. The rough finish on the floor of the base simulates sand on a beach. (Some bases with the identical form are found with a smooth surface. Reins leading from the boy's hand to the turtle are missing on this ring.) Grade B, $350 – 500.

Plate 465

Middletown Plate Co., Number 70. A draped cherub holds a cup and donut up and away from a large rat. Grade C+, $200 – 350.

Plate 467

Van Bergh Silver Plate Co., Number 79. A tiny nude cherub is seated on a rock. Its raised hand holds what appears to be a flower or torch. The base is composed of openwork scrolls. Grade D+, under $200.

1315. Per dozen, $27.00.

Plate 469

Reed & Barton, Number 1315. This is an illustration from the company's 1885 catalog. The drawing shows the dog and Cupid in different positions from the actual napkin ring—an example of the artistic license practiced by illustrators.

Plate 468

Reed & Barton, Number 1315. Cupid reaches for his quiver of arrows. Mounted on the napkin holder are hearts pierced by arrows and tied with a ribbon—which need little explanation. A frisky dog supports the holder. The small oval base is a woodland of ferns and leaves. Grade C+, $200 – 350.

Plate 470

Meriden Britannia Co., Number 182. A nude cherub straddles the top of a barrel napkin holder while a second cherub apparently attempts to push him off. The cherub on the barrel has drapery across his lap. The napkin holder rests on a plain rectangular base elevated on ball feet. Grade B, $350 – 500.

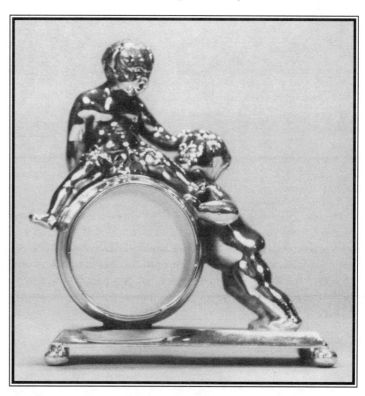

Flowers played an important role in the life of the Victorians. Bouquets, boutonnieres, corsages, flower gardens, and floral decorations are seen illustrated in many Victorian drawings and paintings. Victorians took pride in landscaping their homes, and tending one's flowers was a fashionable pastime. It was also during this era that a special fascination with things from the exotic Orient became the vogue for Americans. These Oriental motifs were often executed with the Occidentals' view of the Far East and as such they are today termed Japonaiserie or Chinoiserie.

If there were subjects which were more typical of everyday life, they were fruits, flowers, berries, butterflies, and fans. This category constituted a universal, no-fail gift, which was suitable for botanists, gardeners, cooks, and Japanophiles, as well as adults and children. Napkin rings within this category were included in just about every manufacturers' line and produced over a long period of time. Though made in large numbers, these rings are quite popular today and are generally reasonable in price.

Plate 471

Left: Meriden Britannia Co., Number 626. Three cherries and four leaves hang from the side of a fluted-edged napkin holder, which is mounted on a square, ball-footed base. Grade C, $200 – 350. **Center:** *Hartford Silver Plate Co., Number 2900.* Two cherries and leaves with a twig decorate a napkin holder, which is elevated by a short pedestal. The base, a large single leaf, rests on ball feet. (It is also found marked Toronto Silver Plate Co., number 1185.) Grade C, $200 – 350. **Right:** *Middletown Plate Co., Number 140.* A leafy branch from which hangs a pear is fastened to the side of a napkin holder elevated by a small pedestal. The base is in the form of a large leaf. (Also found marked Barbour Silver Co., number 2902, and Toronto Silver Plate Co., number 1187.) Grade C, $200 – 350.

Plate 472

Middletown Plate Co., Number 141. Curling branches holding a berry and leaves form a fingerhold handle. The chased napkin holder rests on a low pedestal. The base in the form of a leaf is raised by four small feet. (It is also found marked Toronto Silver Plate Co., number 1170, and Barbour Silver Co., number 2900.) Grade D+, under $200.

Plate 473

Maker not marked, Number 045. (Under the leaf below the napkin holder are the letter W and a diamond-shaped mark.) A large pear is nestled among two leaves with branches. One sizable leaf runs under the napkin holder and becomes its support. The round napkin holder has a hammered finish. (Also found marked Toronto Silver Plate Company, number 1146.) Grade C, $200 – 350.

Plate 474

Maker and number not marked. A large strawberry on three leaves adorns this napkin ring. The napkin holder is embossed with a scene of two fortresses, a tree, and a fountain. The holder itself rests on three smaller leaves. Grade C, $200 – 350.

Plate 475

Left: *Maker and number not marked.* An artful arrangement of a stem with cherries and leaves forms a stand for its hammered-finish napkin holder. A plain area on top provides space for a monogram or message. Grade D+, under $200. **Right:** *Hartford Silver Plate Co., Number 023.* A large pear and branch with one leaf drape over the napkin holder while others hang by the pear. The large leaf-shaped base features an insect near its tip. (This napkin ring is found with other makers' marks and numbers.) Grade C+, $200 – 350.

Plate 476

Toronto Silver Plate Co., Number 1173. An oblique-shaped napkin holder adds interest to three cherries draped on one side. A small square base has a wide decorative fringe-like border. Grade C, $200 – 350.

Plate 477

Standard Silver Co., Ltd., Number 732. Three cherries and leaves drape over one side of a napkin holder which has a leaf-shaped base. (Also found marked Acme Silver Co. with the same number.) Grade C, $200 – 350.

Plate 479

Standard Silver Co. Ltd., Number 733. Grapes topped with a leaf are draped over one side of a wine barrel, which is elevated by a short pedestal. The base in the shape of a grape leaf is elevated by a low, recessed ring. Grade C, $200 – 350.

Plate 478

Maker and number not marked. Grapes in a double row and leaves hang from one side of a napkin holder supported by a round base with a floral design. Grade C, $200 – 350.

Plate 480

Meriden Britannia Co., Number 211. A napkin holder on wheels has a fancy handle, which curves under the holder, and culminates in a rosette. A pretty, detailed butterfly on a ball adorns the handle. Grade B+, $350 – 500.

Plate 481

James W. Tufts, Number 1542. A butterfly rests on a leaf base that ends in a handle. The napkin holder is decorated with a basket-weave design. Grade D+, under $200.

Plate 482

Maker not marked, Number 61. A butterfly lights on top of a napkin holder. Scroll handles decorate the sides and end on a round rocky base. Grade D+, under $200.

Plate 483

Maker and number not marked. A napkin holder rests on a graceful scrolled base that is decorated with bunches of grapes. A large butterfly facing the front and jutting out from the napkin holder is the support for a place card. Grade C, $200 – 350.

Plate 484

Maker and number not marked. A butterfly is mounted on top of the napkin holder, which is supported by a pair of scrolled feet. Grade D+, under $200.

Plate 485

Meriden Silver Plate Co., Number 290. Oriental fans, one on each side, decorate a napkin holder, which is mounted on a square block that rests on an oval, raised base. Grade C, $200 – 350.

Plate 486

Rogers, Smith & Co., Number 209. Two large butterflies rest on a chased, round fan that supports a napkin holder that is of classical Meriden Britannia Co. design. A circular, recessed rim under the base elevates the ring to add importance. Though fairly common, this item is beautifully made and sold for $2.00 wholesale in 1886, a costly sum at the time. (Also found marked Meriden Britannia Co., number 209.) Grade C, $200 –350.

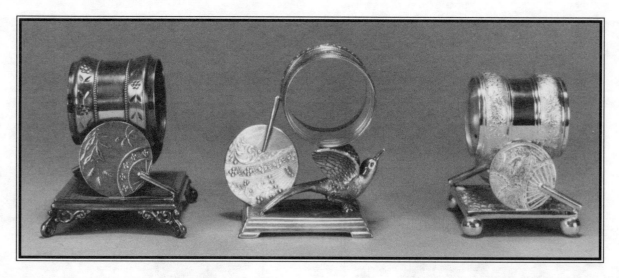

Plate 487

Left: *Simpson, Hall, Miller & Co., Number 053.* A pair of Oriental fans rests on either side of a napkin holder. The square base is elevated by fancy scroll feet. Grade C, $200 – 350. **Center:** *Derby Silver Co., Number 346.* An Oriental fan and a long-tailed bird support a napkin holder with decorated borders. The base is a rectangle with tiered sides. Grade C, $200 – 350. **Right:** *Rogers & Brother, Number 208.* Two Oriental fans support the napkin holder, under which is a butterfly—all mounted on a square, ball-footed base. (Also found marked Meriden Britannia Co. with the same number.) Grade D, under $200.

Plate 488

Simpson, Hall, Miller & Co., Number 213. Forming the napkin holder is a pair of Oriental fans, which are tied with rope containing identical scenes of a Chinese junk boat, bamboo, and mountains. The square, footed base is decorated with a woven design. Grade C, $200 – 350.

Plate 489

Derby Silver Co., Number 335. A pair of large, Oriental fans forms a napkin holder on a raised, tiered oval base. These fans were produced with various designs, using the same number. (Also found illustrated in the catalog, ca. 1870, of Wm. Rogers Mfg. Co., number 6.) Grade C, $200 – 350.

Plate 490

Pairpoint Manufacturing Co., Number not marked. An Oriental fan rests in front of the napkin holder. Three ball feet and the handle of the fan support the ring. Grade D, under $200.

Plate 491

Barbour Bros. Co., Number 9. A calla lily nestled in three leaves adorns the rectangular base edged with an acanthus-leaf design and decorative feet. Grade C, $200 – 350.

Plate 492

Pairpoint Manufacturing Co., Number 6. This is a fetching piece composed of large, fern-like leaves and three-leaf clovers, which elevate the napkin holder on a round raised base. Grade D+, under $200.

Plate 493

Maker not marked, Number 042. Three flowers and a stem with three leaves embrace a child-size napkin holder (one and one-half inch opening). The center section of the holder is prettily decorated with an Oriental design composed of bamboo, a fan, bird, and dragonfly. Grade D+, under $200.

Plate 494

Maker and number not marked. Flat urns with flowers hold the napkin holder above a decorative, square base. Grade C, $200 – 350.

Plate 495

Meriden Britannia Co., Number 168. A lily-leaf base supports a napkin holder on a short pedestal. A lily bud, whose stem forms a handle, decorates one side. Not Meriden's cheapest ring, it is well made and one of its best selling designs judging from the great numbers seen for sale and in collections today. Its wholesale cost was $1.33. (It is shown as number 4 in ca.1888 Simpson, Hall, Miller & Co. wholesale catalog, and available with gold lining at additional cost. In addition, it is shown in the catalog of Benj. Allen & Co., a Chicago wholesale jobber, with prices of $1.62 in silver plate and $1.88 with gold lining.) Grade D+, under $200.

Plate 496

Aurora Silver Plate Co., Number 38. Flowers and leaves, which rest on a round base, support an elevated napkin holder. Grade C, $200 – 350.

Plate 497

Acme Silver Co., Number 723. Flowers and leaves decorate the sides of an embossed napkin holder, which has an appliquéd shield for engraving on top. A lobed pedestal elevates the napkin holder from a plain, rectangular base with ball feet. Grade C, $200 – 350.

Plate 498

Wm. Rogers Mfg. Co., Number 4. A nicely formed large rose with leaves ornaments this ring, which rests on a three-tiered base. Grade C, $200 – 350.

Plate 499

Meriden Britannia Co., Number 298. A large open flower with a sizable leaf that forms the base adorns a napkin holder with ruffled edges. Grade C, $200 – 350.

Plate 500

Left: *Maker and number not marked.* A small napkin holder rests on a branch with a butterfly. Grade D+, under $200. **Right:** *Middletown Plate Co., Number 139.* This napkin ring features a flower on an extended stem that serves as a handle. The base is a formed leaf, upon which is a short pedestal with the napkin holder. (It is also found marked Toronto Silver Plate Co., number 1184.) Grade C, $200 – 350.

Plate 501

Toronto Silver Plate Co., Number 1145. A scalloped-edge leaf decorated with three flowers, and a stem handle are given height by a round ring, recessed under the leaf base plus a pedestal under the napkin holder. (The Toronto catalog shows the leaf base flat, not curled as shown here.) Grade C, $200 – 350.

Plate 502

Meriden Britannia Co., Number 38. A large open flower decorates one side of the napkin holder, while a stem fingerhold centered with a rosette continues into three leaves that form the base. Grade C, $200 – 350.

Plate 504

Middletown Plate Co., Number 96. A scalloped-edge leaf base elevated by a recessed round ring holds a cluster of three small flowers. The stem of the leaf curls to form a fingerhold. Grade C, $200 – 350.

Plate 503

Maker and number not marked. A large rosebud hangs from a stem with three leaves on both sides of a heavy napkin holder. Arched branches with leafy scrolls form a raised base. Grade D+, under $200.

Plate 505

Meriden Silver Plate Co., Number 252. Small, stylized berries drape over a napkin holder that rests on arched leaves, elevating the napkin holder at the center. Grade C+, $200 – 350.

Kate Greenaway, born in 1846, was a shy, English artist and book illustrator known for her original and charming children's books. She first exhibited her art in 1868, and her first successful book was published in 1879 to much praise for her illustrations. Fame followed.

Kate Greenaway's use of clothing drawn from the early nineteenth century caught the fancy of the public. These early styles were both romantic and nostalgic. The popularity of her drawings caused many imitators in Europe and America.

She died in London in 1901, as did Queen Victoria.

The Kate Greenaway-types of figural napkin rings especially capture the tranquility and innocence of small children and, like her books, delight collectors of all ages and gender.

Figural napkin rings after the style of Kate Greenaway are possibly the most highly sought of the figurals today. Unfortunately, this popularity and high prices for the originals have created a market for fakes and reproductions. Special caution must be taken when acquiring these napkin rings.

Infants

Plate 506

Derby Silver Co., Number 335. A Greenaway-type baby in a long dress and wearing a bonnet sits by a decorative napkin holder on a tiered, oval base. Grade B, $350 – 500.

Plate 507

Middletown Plate Co., Number 98. A Greenaway-type baby is seated on a chair. The napkin holder, base, and chair are highly decorated with a plethora of Victorian era ornamentation and flowing lines. Grade A, $500 and up.

Plate 508

Middletown Plate Co., Number 25. A Greenaway-type baby in a long dress and wearing a bonnet kneels on a raised, rectangular base. The baby's hands touch the napkin holder. Grade B, $350 – 500.

Boys

Plate 509

Maker and number not marked. (Located: Toronto Silver Plate Co., Number 1160.) A Greenaway-type boy rides on a dogcart. This makes a rare duo when teamed with the matching girl. Grade A+, $500 and up.

Plate 511

Maker and number not marked. A Greenaway-type boy balances atop a rustic, wooden post fence, which forms the napkin holder. See plate 545. Grade C+, $200 – 350.

Plate 510

Meriden Silver Plate Co., Number 299. A Greenaway-type lad dressed in a sailor suit sits on a fancy, circular base. His hands grasp ropes that encircle the napkin holder and end in tassels. Grade B+, $350 – 500.

Plate 512

James W. Tufts, Number 1598. A Greenaway-type boy stands next to a wooden fence, which forms the napkin holder. The ball-footed oval base has a ribbed edge and is decorated in a geometric pattern. This napkin ring is also found with a higher fence that creates a larger opening for the napkin. The figure may also be found positioned differently although the number is the same. (Caution: This ring has been often reproduced.) Grade B, $350 to 500.

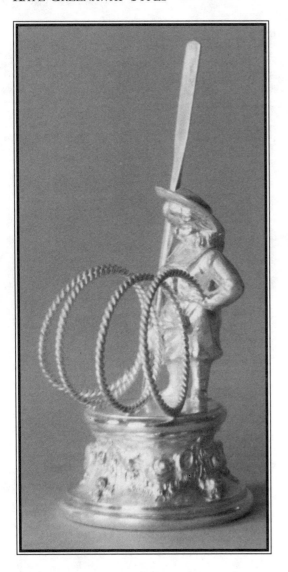

Plate 514

Simpson, Hall, Miller & Co., Number 048. A Greenaway-type boy, manning a pair of oars, sits in a rowboat mounted on a plain, stepped, rectangular base. The maker is known for outstanding original designs, and this napkin ring is proof. They do not come more charming than this one. Grade A+, $500 and up.

Plate 513

Meriden Silver Plate Co., Number 294. Rope spirals form a napkin holder which gives this napkin ring high marks for an original concept. The raised pedestal base is embossed with seashells and sea life. The Greenaway-type sailor boy holds an upright oar, which adds attention to a rare and important napkin ring. Grade A+, $500 and up.

Plate 515

Simpson, Hall, Miller & Co., Number 225. A Greenaway-type boy rides on a horse. The tree bark finish on the napkin holder and an old plank-board road, which forms the base, are reminiscent of an early American scene. This original and appealing design creates a desirable napkin ring. Grade A+, $500 and up.

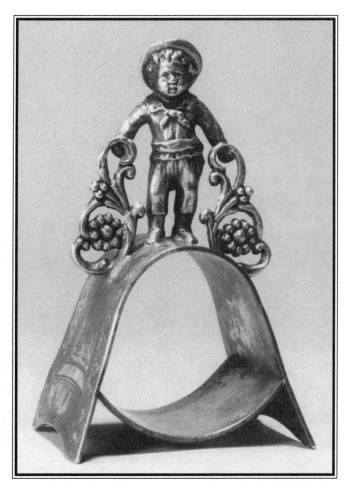

Plate 516

Simpson, Hall, Miller & Co., Number not marked. A Green-away-type boy dressed in a sailor suit and wearing a hat stands on top of a napkin holder. He grasps a pair of scrolled handles that end with rosettes. Grade C, $200 – 350.

Plate 517

Maker and number not marked. (Located: Forbes Silver Co., Number 1022.) A Greenaway-type boy wearing a hat, overalls, and shirt with a ruffled collar stands with hands behind his back. The hexagonal-shaped napkin holder is decorated with a scrolled edge. Grade C+, $200 – 350.

Plate 518

Rogers, Smith & Co., Number 234. A Greenaway-type boy with his arms at his back stands before the napkin holder. This identical figure was produced holding a baseball bat through the crook of the right arm and a ball by his foot. (See Sports chapter. The number differs from above.) Grade C+, $200 – 350.

Plate 519

Maker and number not marked. A Greenaway-type boy stands with hands behind his back before a rope-edged napkin holder. Grade C+, $200 – 350.

Plate 520

James W. Tufts, Number 1601. A Greenaway-type boy holding a ball sits astride a draped-ribbon napkin holder. Decorated with flowers, the holder was designed for monogram engraving. This one is dated May 8, 1884, on one side and contains initials on the opposite. This piece was available in gold plate. (Minus the figure of the boy, this article was marketed with number 1585.) Grade C+, $200 – 350.

Plate 521

James W. Tufts, Number 1611. A Greenaway-type boy dressed in a tasseled cap and jacket with coattails sits atop an oval biscuit box, which serves as the napkin holder. He holds the lid, which provides an ideal space for an engraved name, monogram, or message. The base, which is on ball feet, is oval with a ribbed edge. A fabulous piece! Grade A+, $500 and up.

Plate 522

Hartford Silver Plate Co., Number 030. A Greenaway-type boy, wearing a tasseled cap and knickers with knee socks, sits on a bench in front of a napkin holder. He holds a stick in his right hand. The napkin holder is mounted to the bench with a bolt and fastened with a nut under the base. (Missing is a wire that curls around the stick. It represents a horse whip.) Grade B, $350 – 500.

Plate 523

Left: *Maker and number not marked. (Probably James W. Tufts.)* A Greenaway-type boy and his dog balance an engraved napkin holder on their backs. Grade C+, $200 – 350. **Right:** *James W. Tufts, Number 1617.* A Greenaway-type boy lies on a rectangular base with chamfered corners. This napkin ring with openwork holder was available in gold plate for an extra charge. Grade C+, $200 – 350.

Plate 524

James W. Tufts, Number 1622. A Greenaway-type boy leans against an arched napkin holder. The item protruding from his mouth is sometimes referred to as a whistle. However, it is most likely a cigar, something boys of the 1880s experimented with and is frequently found illustrated in drawings and other objects of the Victorian period. Grade C+, $200 – 350.

Plate 525

Derby Silver Co., Number 378. A Greenaway-type boy in knickers, tasseled cap, and shirt with ruffled collar plays on a slanted board to which are attached reins. A pair of ball feet balances the napkin holder. (The stick in the boy's hand should be straight.) Grade B, $350 – 500.

Plate 526

Maker and number not marked. A small, Greenaway-type boy wearing knickers, a cap, and a shirt with a ruffled collar stands in front of a heavily embossed napkin holder. Grade C, $200 – 350.

Plate 527

Rogers, Smith & Co., Number 251. A very large Greenaway-type boy (4¼" high) wearing a long coat and sporting a big hat is a matching companion to a girl, numbered 250. (These pieces were also produced with the same numbers by Meriden Britannia Co. after it acquired Rogers, Smith & Co. in 1866.) Grade B+, $350 – 500.

Plate 528

Maker and number not marked. (Located: James W. Tufts, Number 1621.) A Greenaway-type boy holds a pair of drumsticks. The narrow napkin holder is designed as a drum. Grade B+, $350 – 500.

Girls

Plate 529

Simpson, Hall, Miller & Co., Number 209. Expensive when new, the Greenaway-type twins on ladders, which are mounted on a rectangular, tiered base, is a rare napkin ring. (The wholesale price in the late 1880s was $2.50 to $3.50, depending on where they were sold and the finish that was ordered.) This is surely an enchanting napkin ring. Grade A+, $500 and up.

Plate 530

Maker not marked, Number 206. (Located: Simpson, Hall, Miller & Co.) A Greenaway-type girl and three owlets on a base composed of branches decorate a wood-grained barrel napkin holder. This imaginative, ca. 1887 object oozes with charm. Traces of gold lining are still seen inside the holder. Grade A+, $500 and up.

Plate 531

Maker and number not marked. A Greenaway-type girl with a pug dog stands in front of the napkin holder. (Reed & Barton produced a similar napkin ring with a different style napkin holder, number 1642.) Grade B, $350 – 500.

Plate 532

Simpson, Hall, Miller & Co., Number 02. This classical Greenaway-type girl is found on many silver-plated figural items. Here, she is standing on a raised, plain, rectangular base with chamfered corners. The napkin holder is elevated by a short pedestal. Grade C+, $200 – 350.

Plate 533

F.B. Rogers Silver Co., Number 244. A Greenaway-type girl facing a seated pug dog is an appealing combination. The oval base is mounted on four ball feet. Grade B+, $350 – 500.

Plate 534

Left: *Wm. Rogers Mfg. Co., Number not marked.* A Greenaway-type girl emerges from the top of this napkin holder. Leaves and cherries act as the base. Grade C+, $200 – 350. **Right:** *Simpson, Hall, Miller & Co. Number 039.* A prized combination of a slender dog, a doghouse, and a Greenaway-type girl gives this piece special favor with buyers. The base is a simple, plain, tiered rectangle. (Missing from the girl's right hand is a crop or leash.) Grade A, $500 and up.

Plate 535

Left: *Toronto Silver Plate Co., Number 1155.* A Greenaway-type girl, wearing a bonnet and with an apron over her dress, pushes a napkin holder with a scalloped edge. The plain base is a rectangle with half-circle ends. Grade C+, $200 – 350. **Right:** *Maker and number not marked.* This ring has the identical figure and napkin holder as the one on the left, but is minus a base. Grade C, $200 – 350.

Plate 536

Rockford Silver Plate Co., Number 120. A Greenaway-type girl stands on the sloping edge of a beautiful, rectangular base. It is covered, as is the napkin holder, with profuse ornamentation popular during the Victorian period. A view of the back of this napkin ring shows the Japonaiserie decoration. Grade B+, $350 – 500.

Plate 537

A view of the back of the plate 536 napkin ring shows the Japonaiserie decoration. Grade B+, $350 – 500.

Plate 538

Wm. Rogers Mfg. Co., Number 285. A Greenaway-type girl pushes a barrel napkin holder down a ramp. Grade B, $350 – 500.

Plate 539

Maker not marked. Number 032. (Located: Simpson, Hall, Miller & Co.) A Greenaway-type girl pushes a highly decorated napkin holder. The number may be located either on the bottom of the girl's foot or the bottom of her dress. Grade C+, $200 – 350.

Plate 540

Simpson, Hall, Miller & Co., Number 031. A cord around the neck of the Greenaway-type girl fastens to the napkin holder, which represents a drum. A second drumstick elevates the napkin holder at its base. Grade B+, $350 – 500.

Plate 541

Simpson, Hall, Miller & Co., Number 205. A Greenaway-type girl, holding a toy rifle, stands in front of the napkin holder on a square base with decorative scrolled feet. Patriotic games were accepted as play before the period of war protesters and out-of-favor children's military toys. Grade A, $500 and up.

Plate 542

Maker not marked. Number 030. (Located: Simpson, Hall, Miller & Co.) A Greenaway-type girl pulls a two-wheeled cart, which supports a highly decorated napkin holder. The combination of Greenaway types and wheeled napkin rings is very desirable. Grade A, $500 and up.

Plate 543

Simpson, Hall, Miller & Co., Number 027. Branches and leaves rest on a scalloped, round base with ball feet. A Greenaway-type girl holding a stick plays with a baby girl aloft in the tree limbs. Grade A+, $500 and up.

Plate 544

Maker not marked, Number 1150. A Greenaway-type girl rides on a cart drawn by a dog. This attractive wheeled piece is a companion to a boy, dog, and cart. (Pictured in the 1888 catalog of the Toronto Silver Plate Co., this item is listed as number 1159. The difference in numbers leads to speculation that this napkin ring was produced or sold by another company—a common practice. Or it is possibly a typographical error inasmuch as number 9 is close to zero on the typewriter.) Grade A+, $500 and up.

Plate 545

Maker and number not marked. A Greenaway-type girl balances on a rustic wood fence. This is one of a series of napkin rings without tubular napkin holders. (This style of napkin rings has not been located in original old catalogs, and to date none has been found with manufacturer's marks.) Grade C+, $200 – 350.

Plate 546

Derby Silver Co., Number 316. A Greenaway-type girl dressed in a bonnet, long dress, and cape is seated on a small, square flat base next to the napkin holder. Grade B, $350 – 500.

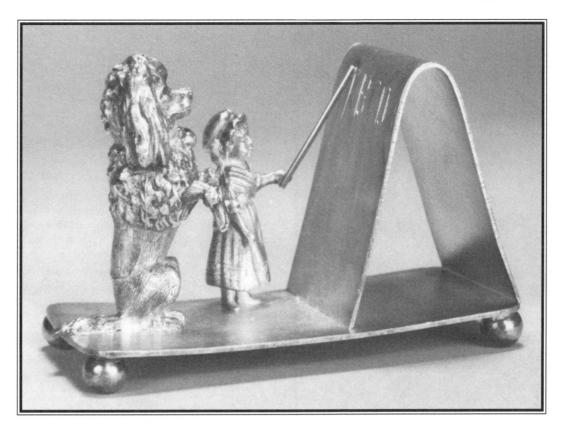

Plate 547

James W. Tufts, Number 1669. A Greenaway-type girl instructs a large poodle in the ABC's from a blackboard that forms the napkin holder. This is a most impressive figural napkin ring because of its size and subject. An original design, it was made toward the end of Tufts's production of napkin rings. The base is 4⅜" long by 2¼" wide. Grade A+, $500 and up.

Plate 548

Maker and number not marked. (Probably Wilcox Silver Plate Co.) A small, kneeling Greenaway-type figure tries on a top hat. Although this is a child-size napkin holder, it is desirable because of the subject matter. Grade C+, $200 – 350.

Plate 549

Rogers, Smith & Co., Number 250. A large Greenaway-type girl dressed in a long coat and bonnet and holding a muff is a companion to a boy in a long coat and top hat. These figures were also produced as salt and pepper shakers, both with and without napkin holders attached. (Rogers, Smith & Co. was acquired by Meriden Britannia Co., and this napkin ring is found with either companies' mark.) Grade B+, $350 – 500.

Plate 550

Meriden Silver Plate Co., Number 0238. A Greenaway-type girl with a staff drives a pair of geese held by reins. *The Goose Girl*, written by the Grimm Brothers, was probably the inspiration for this napkin ring. The oval base is pressed metal with acanthus leaves and flowers in its border. Grade A+, $500 and up.

Plate 551

Meriden Silver Plate Co., Number 0236. A Greenaway-type girl pets a goat held by a rope. She stands next to a napkin holder that rests on the edge of a raised, oval base of pressed metal with acanthus leaves and flowers in its border. This napkin ring is possibly a depiction of Heidi from the children's book of the same name. Grade A+, $500 and up.

Plate 552

J. A. Babcock & Co., Number not marked. A Greenaway-type girl holding a stick plays with a kitten, which stands on its hind legs. The raised rectangular base has an embossed border design. Grade B, $350 – 500.

Plate 554

Maker and number not marked. A seated Greenaway-type girl holding the ribbon ties to her bonnet is joined at the arm to a child-siz napkin holder. Grade C+, $200 – 350.

Plate 553

Meriden Britannia Co., Number 130. A Greenaway-type girl wearing a bonnet sits atop the napkin holder which rests on a pyramidal base. (Meriden produced a series using this identical base and holder but with different figures on top. All carry number 130, including one with just the base and holder and no figure.) Grade C+, $200 – 350.

Plate 555

Maker and number not marked. (Located: Derby Silver Co., Number 113.) A Greenaway-type girl of fine quality is seated on a forked and curving branch which supports the napkin holder. The figure is an exceptionally heavy, solid casting. Grade B, $350 – 500.

Plate 556

Maker and number not marked. (Possibly Derby Silver Co.) A big sister Greenaway-type figure is a hollow casting, which is open at the base. She wears a long coat and a hat trimmed with feathers. The holder is small in size (1⅝" in diameter.) Grade C+, $200 – 350.

Plate 557

Left: *Derby Silver Co. Number 314.* A Greenaway-type little sister (2¼" tall), who wears a long coat and hat trimmed with feathers, carries a muff. A playful, barking dog is mounted on the other side of the napkin holder. Grade B, $350 – 500. **Right:** *Derby Silver Co., Number 314.* A Greenaway-type big sister (2⅝" tall) wears an identical outfit as the little sister. The same dog is also featured here. (Big and little sisters are both marked with identical numbers.) Grade B, $350 – 500.

Plate 558

Maker not marked. Number 380. (Probably Derby Silver Co.) Big sister and little sister Greenaway-type figures are placed on either side of a napkin holder with a mottled finish and with a plain area on top for a monogram. (The catalog number is found at the base of big sister.) Grade B+, $350 – 500.

Plate 559

Homan Silver Plate Co., Number 31. A Greenaway-type girl wearing a hat trimmed with feathers and a long coat and carrying a muff stands alongside a napkin holder decorated with a geometric grid-work design. A barking dog is on the opposite side of the oval base. Grade B+, $350 – 500.

Plate 560

Homan Silver Plate Co., Number 31. A view of the back shows the dog.

Plate 561

James W. Tufts, Number 1615. A Greenaway-type girl wearing a hat trimmed with feathers and a long coat and carrying a muff stands next to a pretty napkin holder with an openwork design. The plain, raised, rectangular base has cutout corners. Grade B+, $350 – 500.

Combinations of Boys and Girls

Plate 562

Simpson, Hall, Miller & Co., Number 037. A girl pushes a boy on a sled. Both figures follow the Greenaway style. The napkin ring is unique because the square napkin holder is cleverly integrated in the design with the sled. A highly sought piece due to the subject matter as well as the Greenaway popularity. Grade A+, $500 and up.

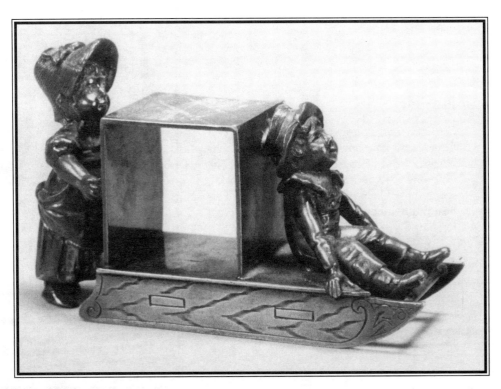

Plate 563

Simpson, Hall, Miller & Co., Number 040. A rectangular napkin holder represents a brick wall, over which a small girl standing on a stool looks at a boy. The words found on the base of this important napkin ring with Greenaway-type figures read: "Over the Garden Wall." This was a popular song of the Victorian period, written by George D. Fox and taken from a stage production entitled *Ring Up the Curtain.* A wonderful and original design in which the napkin slips through the wall. Grade A+, $500 and up.

Plate 564

Simpson, Hall, Miller, and Co., Number 036. A Greenaway-type boy reads a book while seated on a lovely, ornate, Victorian chair. The Greenaway-type girl peeks from behind, a scene most likely copied from real life. This beautifully modeled pair is superb, creating a fetching scene. Grade A+, $500 and up.

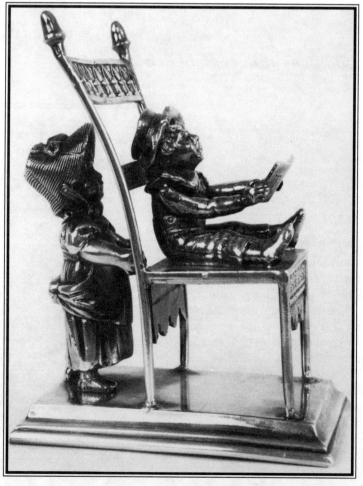

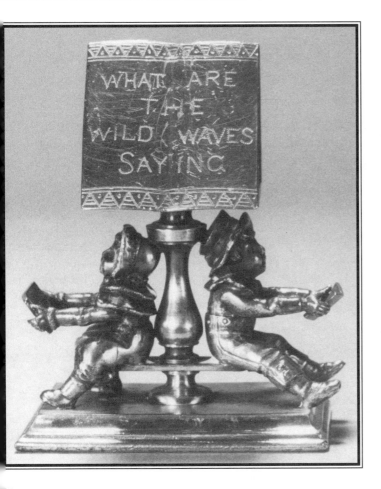

Plate 566

Simpson, Hall, Miller & Co., Number 038. The song book, which forms the elevated, triangular napkin holder, reads "Little Buttercup," another popular song of the Victorian period. This Greenaway-type napkin ring is a variation of "What Are the Wild Waves Saying." Both rings use the same number. Grade A+, $500 and up.

Plate 565

Simpson, Hall, Miller & Co., Number 038. One of the most rare of the Greenaway-type napkin rings, a back-to-back boy and girl holding books sit on a ledge under a triangular napkin holder. Engraved on the elevated holder is "What Are the Wild Waves Saying," a popular Victorian song first published in 1850. (Signs of gold wash are still visible on parts of this wonderful ring.) Grade A+, $500 and up.

Plate 567

Simpson, Hall, Miller & Co., Number 029. Greenaway-type children play on a teeter-totter, a nostalgic rendition composed of three tree limbs, which support the board. Sometimes this ring is found missing its plain, rectangular base with half-circle ends, but it is shown in the manufacturer's catalogs only with the base, never without one. It is also shown in the 1888 Toronto Silver Plate Co. catalog, number 1158.) Grade A+, $500 and up.

Plate 568

*Simpson, Hall, Miller &
Co., Number 041.* The
Greenaway-type Jack and
Jill are depicted falling
down the hill, which is
also the napkin holder.
Under Jack's legs is the
bucket. Grade A+, $500
and up.

Plate 569

James W. Tufts, Number 1667. Jack and Jill stand on a charming and unique version of the hill, represented by a folded piece of metal that, of course, holds the napkin. Their names are engraved on the holder.
Grade A+, $500 and up.

Plate 570

Southington Cutlery Co., Number 102. Greenaway-type children play on a sliding board, which forms the napkin holder. The girl stands on a ladder with ball feet, which serves as balance for the ring. This clever design makes it a cherished collectible. (Southington operated from 1886 to 1893, when it was acquired by Meriden Britannia Co., which did not continue the use of the Southington name.) Grade A+, $500 and up.

Plate 571

Meriden Silver Plate Co., Number 0237. A Greenaway-type girl withholds the stick from a little crying boy, who wants it for his hoop. The hoop and stick were popular playthings during the last quarter of the nineteenth century. The border of the raised, pressed-metal oval base is decorated with acanthus leaves and flowers. (The hoop, which is in a precarious position, is often missing, causing collectors to incorrectly name this piece "Spare the Rod.") Grade A+, $500 and up.

Plate 572

Maker and number not marked. A Greenaway-type boy and girl flank each side of a rustic wood fence napkin holder. (This napkin ring has not so far been located in manufacturer's or jobber's catalogs.) Grade A, $500 and up.

Plate 573

Left and right: *James W. Tufts, Number 1597.* Two winsome, Greenaway-type napkin rings with similarities and differences, carry the same manufacturer's number. A young lady holds a parasol as a small boy plays with a stick and hoop. The major difference between the two rings is the boy on the left who is smaller than the boy on the right and who wears an entirely different outfit. In addition, the parasol on the right has ribs, which are pronounced on the outer surface, and the positions of the napkin holders do not match. Either version is a most welcomed addition to a collection. Grade A+, $500 and up.

Plate 574

James W. Tufts, Number 1597. A front view of the napkin ring above.

Plate 575

Simpson, Hall, Miller & Co., Number 047. A Greenaway-type girl teaches two young Greenaway-type children the ABC's from a blackboard, which forms the napkin holder. The rectangular base is elevated by ball feet, and its border is decorated with alternating rosettes and foliate embellishments. It is rare to find a napkin ring with three figures. Grade A+, $500 and up.

Women

Plate 576

James W. Tufts, Number 1590. A Greenaway-type young woman holding a parasol stands on one side of a scalloped-edged napkin holder, which is elevated by a pedestal. A crouching dog peers from the opposite side. (This pair of figures was produced by Tufts with a perfume bottle and its holder, number 3054.) Grade A+, $500 and up.

Plate 577

Wilcox Silver Plate Co., Number 4336. A Greenaway-type woman, wearing a large hat and long dress, sits on a tuffet and supports the napkin holder on her knees. The raised base, which is round, is embossed with an ornate design. Grade A, $500 and up.

Plate 578

Derby Silver Co., Number 381. A Greenaway-type lady stands with one foot forward. She wears an 1820s dress, bonnet, and draped shawl—typical of Kate Greenaway's drawings. A scroll design decorates the hem of her dress. This is a nicely modeled figure. Grade A, $500 and up.

MARINE LIFE

Before air conditioning, there were few Victorians who did not visit a lake or beach during the heat of summer and experience first hand the wonders of marine life. What boy could resist catching a frog or a turtle? Children have always been fascinated with things that crawl, hop, or swim. Of all the marine life figural napkin rings produced, only the dolphin has, at times, an exaggerated form, leaving to speculation that perhaps the designers never actually viewed one in real life.

Beavers

Plate 579

Left: *Acme Silver Co., Number 758.* A large and small beaver balance a beautiful, openwork napkin holder, which is embossed with a bird and flowers. The base is a large maple leaf. Grade C+, $200 – 350. **Right:** *Toronto Silver Plate Co., Number 1110.* The beaver and maple leaf are indigenous to Canada and were a popular motif of napkin rings produced there. The beaver sits on top of a branch that connects to a maple-leaf base, which securely anchors the napkin holder. Grade C+, $200 – 350.

Dolphins

Plate 580

Pairpoint Manufacturing Co., Number 30. A pair of dolphins supports a napkin holder by their tails. A knife rest connects the heads. Grade C+, $200 – 350.

Plate 581

Southington Cutlery Co., Number 32. A dolphin with its head resting on an oval base decorated with a seashore motif joins the embossed napkin holder by its tail. Grade C, $200 – 350.

Plate 582

Left: *New Haven Silver Plate Co., Number 262.* A child sits on the tail of a dolphin held by reins. The napkin holder rests on an oval base decorated to resemble the seashore. Grade C, $200 – 350. **Right:** *Maker and number not marked.* A child sits astride a dolphin while holding its tail with one arm. (The right hand may have held reins or a trident.) Grade C, $200 – 350.

Frogs

Plate 583

Maker not marked, Number 040. (Located: Pairpoint Manufacturing Co.) A large frog with glass eyes peers back at a fly on top of a napkin holder with a hammered finish. (Also shown in the Toronto Silver Plate Co. catalog, number 1169.) Grade B, $350 – 500.

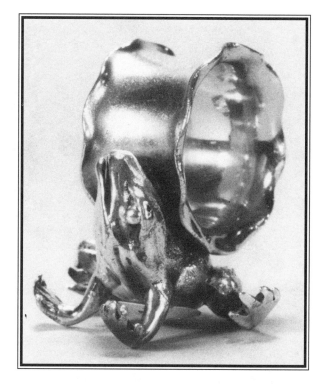

Plate 584

Maker and number not marked. A large frog peers up at a narrow fluted-edged napkin holder, which is mounted on its back. (The frog is the identical casting as Pairpoint, number 040, which has glass eyes, but this one does not.) Grade C+, $200 – 350.

Plate 585

Southington Cutlery Co., Number 35. A large frog leaps beneath the napkin holder, which is attached to the frog's back. The base is formed of overlapping leaves. Grade C+, $200 – 350.

Plate 586

Maker and number not marked. A tiny frog sits on an undulating leaf, which serves as a base for the napkin holder with an engraved flower design. Grade C, $200 – 350.

Plate 587

Meriden Britannia Co., Number 238. A small frog supports a leaf, which holds a fly. The napkin holder is soldered to one end of the leaf. Grade C, $200 – 350.

Plate 588

Aurora Silver Plate Co., Number 37. A small frog perches atop a plain napkin holder, which is supported by a round base of woodland flora. Grade C, $200 – 350.

Plate 589

Maker and number not marked. A frog dressed in clothing sits on a leaf base with its back to the napkin holder. The frog holds a branch with cherries. Grade C+, $200 – 350.

Plate 590

Shelton Bros. & Co., Number 110. A frog wearing boots pushes a napkin holder with a fluted and beaded edge. A butterfly is mounted at the narrow end of the leaf base. Grade C, $200 – 350.

Plate 591

Reed & Barton, Number 1475. A frog dressed in a jacket and standing on a leaf base holds a pair of drumsticks over a napkin holder designed as a drum. Grade C+, $200 – 350.

Plate 592

Reed & Barton, Number 1515. This is an illustration from the 1885 Reed & Barton catalog.

Shells

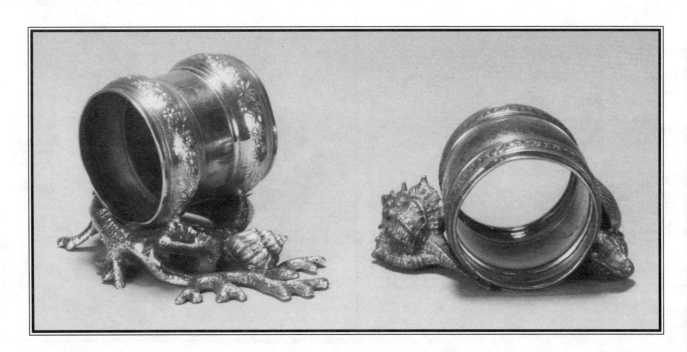

Plate 593

Left: *Meriden Britannia Co. Number 227.* A section of coral holding a small shell forms the base for the napkin holder, which is one of Meriden Britannia's most classical shapes. Grade C, $200 – 350. **Right:** *Meriden Silver Plate Co., Number 0241.* Seashells on each side of the napkin holder serve as both decoration and base. Grade D+, under $200.

Turtles

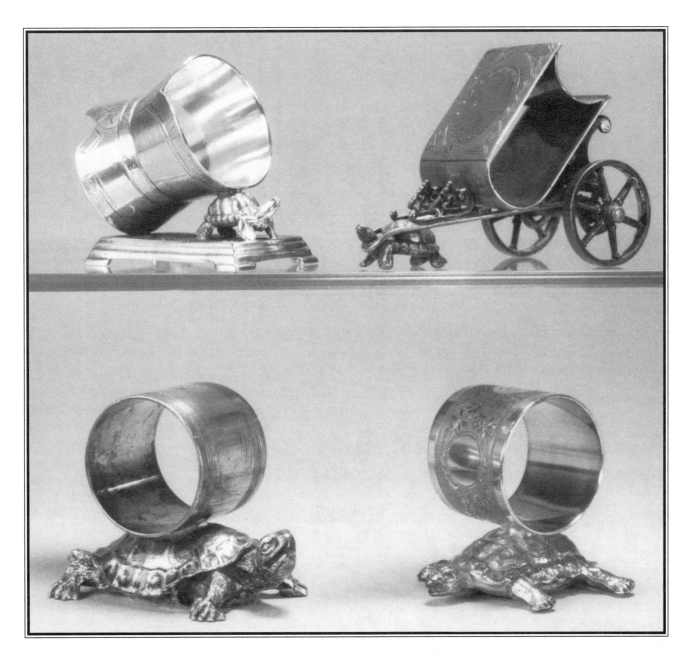

Plate 594

Left: *Derby Silver Co., Number 340.* A tiny turtle supports a napkin holder, which resembles a cinched waist with a belt. A stepped-up, small rectangular base is decorated with field flowers. (Also found marked Rogers & Brother.) Grade C, $200 – 350. **Right:** *Maker not marked, Number 347. (Located Derby Silver Co.)* See next photograph. **Lower left:** *Pairpoint Manufacturing Co., Number 51.* The marks are found on the front feet of this large turtle, which has a hollow body and solid cast feet. The turtle carries the napkin holder on its back. Grade B, $350 – 500. **Lower Right:** *Meriden Britannia Co., Number 193.* A medium-sized turtle supports a napkin holder decorated with tiny flowers and leaves. This holder has three coin-shaped monogram spaces. Grade C+, $200 – 350.

Plate 596

Maker not marked, Number 945. (Located: Reed & Barton.) A turtle balances a beautifully embossed napkin holder on its back. Grade C, $200 – 350.

Plate 595

Maker not marked, Number 347. (Located: Derby Silver Co.) A small turtle pulls a book-shaped napkin holder, which rests on shafts decorated with scrolls, ending in wheels. Does this ring suggest a slow reader? Grade A+, $500 & up.

Plate 597

Meriden Silver Plate Co., Number 216. A pair of matching, small turtles on an elevated, round base support a napkin holder. Grade C, $200 – 350.

MILITARY

hile military napkin rings is a small category, they were nevertheless produced by a few manufacturers. Because women were the primary shoppers during Victorian times, it is suspected that they avoided purchases that related to guns and war. However, patriotism was the theme of some of the military napkin rings. Not all guns were produced for war; some were hunting rifles.

Plate 598

Meriden Silver Plate Co., Number 0260. A Civil War soldier in uniform stands with his rifle next to a napkin holder decorated as a drum. Grade B, $350 – 500.

245

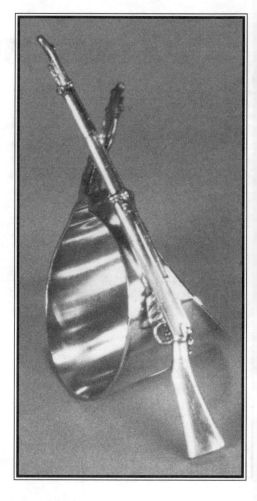

Plate 599

Meriden Britannia Co., Number 335. Crossed rifles support a napkin holder with embossed designs and open scrollwork borders. (Meriden Britannia Co. produced this napkin ring with a napkin holder of a different design.) Grade C+, $200 – 350.

Plate 600

Maker and number not marked. Crossed rifles flank a napkin holder, which narrows at its top. Grade C, $200 – 350.

Plate 601

Meriden Britannia Co. Number 642. "The (Maple Leaf) Forever" motto is printed below crossed swords on the napkin holder. (This is a souvenir of Canada, produced by the Canadian branch of Meriden Britannia Co.) Grade D, under $200.

Plate 602

Toronto Silver Plate Co., Number 1137. A conquistador holding a firearm stands by a napkin holder elevated by two short pedestals. The raised, ornate, rectangular, footed base adds importance and interest to this napkin ring. The napkin holder has an applied monogram shield. Grade B, $350 – 500.

Plate 603

Maker not marked, Number 291. (Located: Meriden Silver Plate Co.) A pair of saddlebags with two swords on each side form the base of the napkin holder, which has a bulbous center. Grade C+, $200 – 350.

Victorians had an undeniable attraction to an eclectic mix of styles, borrowing from every past civilization. They traveled widely abroad and had a great interest in Roman, Etruscan, Greek, and Egyptian architecture, statuary, paintings, furniture, and other decorative arts of antiquity. The designs of the Orient were also part of their creative energy after missionaries and travelers returned home from Japan and India bringing with them objects, drawings, and stories of these areas.

In analyzing Victoriana, thoughts are associated with scrolls, swags, flowers, tassels, and a profusion of highly embellished designs given to rich adornment—everything that is synonymous with excess. The Victorians had a penchant for pattern on pattern.

Where the napkin ring has no category in particular, it has been included in this chapter. For example, wishbones (without chickens), the fireman's hat (which incidentally is the only original one produced that has surfaced to date), horseshoes (without horses), and all those figural napkin rings with gew-gaws.

Manufacturers tried to cover every subject that was marketable. Certainly there are many more bibelots and miscellanea than are shown here.

Plate 604

Pairpoint Manufacturing Co., Number 81. A large fireman's hat rests against the napkin holder. The square base has a design that simulates earth. (Fire memorabilia collectors vie for this napkin ring, making it difficult to find.) Grade A, $500 and up.

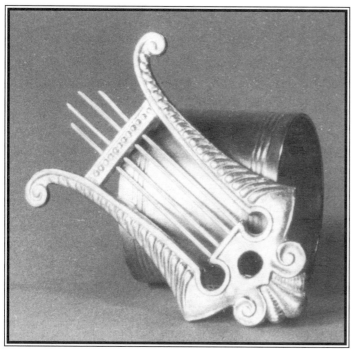

Plate 605

Maker and number not marked. A lyre anchors a napkin holder in place. (Note: The lyre is in its correct position.) Grade D+, under $200.

Plate 606

Maker and number not marked. Substantial, andiron-shaped legs support a napkin holder embellished with an overall intricate design, except for a plain, monogram space on the top. A chevron pattern trims the borders. Grade D, under $200.

Plate 607

Wilcox Silver Plate Co., Number 4347. Wishbones are placed on each end of a triangular-shaped napkin holder engraved with "Best Wishes." This napkin ring is gold-plated. Grade D, under $200.

Plate 608

Maker and number not marked. Leaves decorate large graceful scrolls composed of rustic limbs, creating a base, which is an artful arrangement. Bars at each end of the scrolls serve as knife rests. Grade C+, $200 – 350.

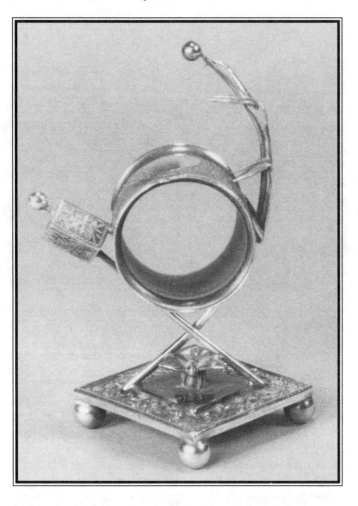

Plate 610

Rogers, Smith & Co., Number 313. This base, like the napkin holder, is pressed metal with cast ball feet and cast fretwork circles that decorate the sides. Grade D, under $200.

Plate 609

Meriden Britannia Co., Number 210. A branch of bamboo and a mikosi (a miniature, Oriental shrine carried during festivities) crisscross under the napkin holder. The square base with ball feet has a butterfly in its center. Grade C, $200 – 350.

Plate 611

Maker and number not marked. (Located: Derby Silver Co., Number 304.) A book-shaped napkin holder is held by an easel, the legs decorated with leaves both front and back. Grade C, $200 – 350.

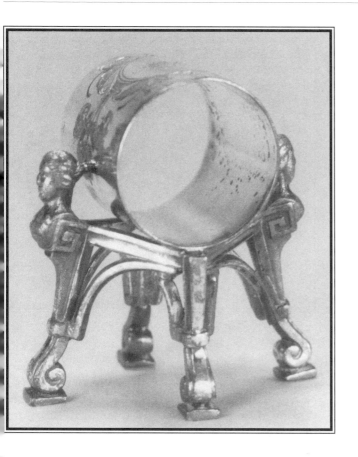

Plate 613

James W. Tufts, Number 1593. A highly decorated napkin holder rests on a log with outcropping branches on either side. A round, mounded base is decorated with woodland motifs. Grade D+, unde $200.

Plate 612

Maker not marked, Number 65. A napkin holder rests on a table-like base with scrolled feet, which curve inward. Human busts top two of the supports. Grade C, $200 – 350.

Plate 614

Toronto Silver Plate Co., Number 78. A triangular napkin holder, engraved "Good Luck," supports a pair of horseshoes on either side. Grade D+, under $200.

Plate 615

James W. Tufts, Number 1540. A large horseshoe, which is embossed "Bonheur" (meaning happiness or good fortune), surmounts the napkin holder, which rests on an oval, ball-footed base covered with geometric designs. Grade C, $200 – 350.

Plate 616

Maker and number not marked. (Located: Pairpoint Manufacturing Co., Number 64.) This heavy and substantial napkin holder has an attached horseshoe. (An identical napkin holder is used by Pairpoint on other rings, which are marked.) Grade D, under $200.

Plate 617

Meriden Silver Plate Co., Number 225. A top hat and glove—or is it a hat in hand?—rest on a square, flat base with cutout corners. The open top hat makes an original napkin holder. Grade C, $200 – 350.

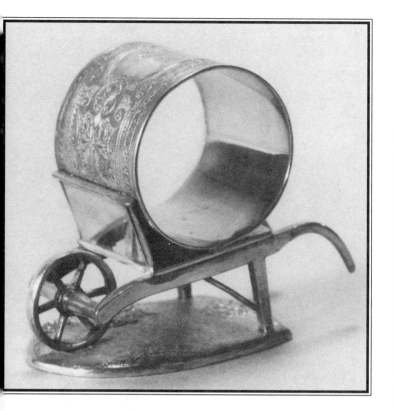

Plate 619

Plate 618

James W. Tufts, Number 1537. This wheelbarrow, mounted on a shield-shaped base that is decorated with earth and flowers, is considered a "wheeled" napkin ring by collectors. (The manufacturer's mark on this piece is on a "coin," although the mark may be found stamped. It wholesaled for $1.75 in silver plate and $2.00 with gold. Tufts produced a simpler wheelbarrow with less workmanship, which sold for a few pennies less, number 1535.) Grade C+, $200 – 350.

Rockford Silver Plate Co., Number 102. A beautiful, heavily embossed napkin holder decorated with Japonaiserie is fastened by leafy scrolled braces. The rectangular base features sloped ends and is decorated with the same motifs. Grade C, $200 – 350.

Plate 620

Pairpoint Manufacturing Co., Number not marked. A napkin holder is mounted on a fanciful wheelbarrow, which has a pretty flower design in the wheel. Grade C, $200 – 350.

Plate 621

Maker and number not marked. A patterned band of ribbon, a simple form, creates a napkin holder. Grade D, under $200.

Plate 622

Simpson, Hall, Miller & Co., Number not marked.
Stylized, winged griffins are framed as parts of the
handle of the napkin ring. The round base is made
of pressed metal. (The maker's mark is on a coin.)
Grade D+, under $200.

Plate 623

Bridgeport Silver Co., Number 214. Griffinesque figures form leg
ending in scrolled feet and support a heavily embossed napkin
holder and lower shelf with cutout sides. Grade C, $200 – 350.

Plate 624

Meriden Silver Plate Co., Number 244. A hand
with flowers decorates a removable band that
secures the cut-glass napkin holder. The band
is fastened beneath the base by a wing nut
over a bolt that extends from the band. The
glass addition to a metal figural napkin ring is
unique; this one wholesaled for $2.50 in the
mid-1880s. (This glass napkin holder was also
used by Derby Silver Co. on a figural napkin
ring.) Grade C, $200 – 350.

Plate 626

James W. Tufts, Number 1636. A napkin holder is incorporated into the form of a clothes iron. Grade D+, under $200.

Plate 625

Meriden Silver Plate Co., Number 264. A griffin proudly sits at the top of the napkin holder, mounted on a ball elevated by a domed, open base. The base gives this ring its height, which adds importance. (Note: The griffin should have wings, which are missing on this example.) Grade C, $200 – 350.

Plate 627

I.J. Sharick, Number 239. The hammered finish of this napkin ring distinguishes this artist's palette and napkin holder. The base is elevated by a recessed, short, round ring. (The mark is most likely a retailer from Albuquerque, New Mexico; the location is marked on the base. This identical piece with the addition of small flowers draped on the napkin holder and a fly on the palette is found in the 1886–87 Meriden Britannia Co. catalog with the same number and available with gold lining for extra cost. This ring is also found marked Rogers, Smith & Co., Number 239.) Grade C, $200 – 350.

Plate 628

Left: *Simpson, Hall, Miller & Co., Number 97.* A large, red, faceted stone, which is held by prongs, is mounted atop a simulated bracelet. The base has four, small ball feet. Grade D+, under $200. **Right:** *Meriden Silver Plate Co., Number not marked.* A clothes iron, its handle forming the napkin holder, is engraved with scrolls of flowers and leaves. Grade D+, under $200.

Plate 629

Maker and number not marked. A valise, which forms the napkin holder, has an applied handle that is fixed to the side. Grade D, under $200.

Plate 630

Maker not marked, Number 329. (Located: Derby Silver Co.) A valise, which forms the napkin holder, has a stationary upright handle and small, flat rectangular base. A clasp and straps decorate the ring. (Also found marked Wm. Rogers & Son, number 5, and Winsted Silver Plate Co., number 5.) Grade D+, under $200.

Plate 631

Maker and number not marked. (Possibly Reed & Barton.) A barrel with staves forms a napkin holder, which is supported by branches and leaves. Grade D, under $200.

Plate 632

Wm. Rogers Mfg. Co., Number 277. A form, which resembles an ornate nutcracker, surrounds a heavily embossed napkin holder supported at both ends by moths. Grade C+, $200 – 350.

Plate 633

Wilcox Silver Plate Co., Number 4393. A violin leans against the napkin holder engraved with leaves. The sheet-music base with curled corners is engraved "Old Times." Three ball feet elevate the base. Grade C+, $200 – 350.

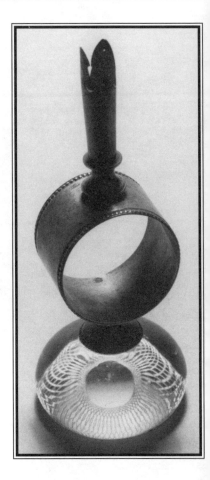

Plate 635

Maker and number not marked. An unusual combination of a napkin holder with what appears to be a bud vase holder mounted on top and, on the bottom, a glass paperweight base. The short bud vase probably held a glass insert. Grade D+, under $200.

Plate 634

Bridgeport Silver Co., Number 208. A napkin holder hangs from connecting hooks in a cage formed by wires ending in scrolled feet. A flower decorates the top while an octagonal shelf completes the base. Grade C+, $200 – 350.

Plate 636

James W. Tufts, Number 1620. An infant lies in a cradle which actually rocks. One foot of the infant protrudes from the covers. The open center of the cradle holds the napkin. This ring is engraved "Mother." An enchanting piece. Grade A, $500 and up.

Plate 637

Maker and number not marked. (Located: James W. Tufts, Number 1589.) A different concept for a napkin holder is this book, which may represent a family album or Bible. A clasp adds interest to this ring. Grade D, under $200.

Plate 638

Middletown Plate Co., Number 164. The napkin holder, which is decorated with scrolled edges, is engraved "Best Wishes." A bow and quiver of arrows rest on a heart-shaped base elevated by ball feet. Grade D+, under $200.

Plate 639

Maker and number not marked. A hand, which holds flowers, decorates the top of the napkin holder, supported by solid braces with cutout trim. Grade D, under $200.

Plate 640

Pairpoint Manufacturing Co., Number 53. Fancy, openwork sides join to form a trapezoid-shaped napkin holder, supported by four ball feet. Grade D, under $200.

What a wonderful category this is! It includes people in various occupations, at work, at play and wearing a variety of clothing. Some are lovingly recording events of daily life, such as the lady watering flowers or the baker carrying a flour barrel. While silver-plated figural napkin rings are primarily an American product, people from foreign lands are depicted. For example, Egypt, Europe, and Asia reflected the Victorians' interest in exotic lands and travel. From this large selection of napkin rings, the buyer was surely able to find a suitable theme to match a recipient. The number and variety of messages, monograms, and names engraved on many of the rings indicate that this category was an immensely popular gift item.

Boys

Plate 641

Meriden Silver Plate Co., Number 0232. A young boy crawling on hands and knees peers from behind the napkin holder as he successfully snares a bunny. Both the boy and the napkin holder are attached to the base with bolts and nuts. Grade A+, $500 and up.

Plate 642

Left: *Meriden Silver Plate Co., Number 274.* A boy on hands and knees approaches a bird's nest and encounters the fury of a mother bird. The oval base, which has a scalloped edge, is heavily decorated. Grade C+, $200 – 350. **Right:** *Meriden Silver Plate Co., Number 269.* A boy on hands and knees peers into a nest of bird's eggs. The round, raised base is decorated with a ridge-designed border. Grade C+, $200 – 350.

Plate 643

Maker and number not marked. (Probably Meriden Silver Plate Co. or Reed & Barton.) A crawling boy carries a wide napkin holder on his back. (This figure was also produced carrying a narrow napkin holder.) Grade C+, $200 – 350.

Plate 644

Maker and number not marked. (Located: Reed & Barton, Number 480.) A crawling boy carries a narrow napkin holder on his back. (The manufacturer utilized this figure in many other designs.) Grade C+, $200 – 350.

Plate 645

Meriden Silver Plate Co., Number 248. A crawling boy carries a napkin holder, which is decorated as a drum and has mounted on it a pair of drumsticks. The flat octagonal base has a polished border. Grade C+, $200 – 350.

Plate 646

Meriden Silver Plate Co., Number 250. A boy crouches on an octagonal base with hands against the napkin holder. (This figure is the same as the crawling boys produced by Meriden Silver Plate Co.) Grade C+, $200 – 350.

Plate 648

Wilcox Silver Plate Co., Number 01549. A young, barefoot boy lying on his back balances on his hands and knees a napkin holder with a fluted edge. The oval base is decorated as a shield with stars and stripes. Grade B, $350 – 500.

Plate 647

Meriden Britannia Co., Number 155. A young lad, wearing a hat and knickers and with sleeves of his shirt rolled up, carries a napkin holder on his back by a rope. Grade C+, $200 – 350.

Plate 649

Meriden Britannia Co., Number 171. A young lad pushes a barrel-shaped napkin holder that is engraved "100 yds. under 13/ 2nd prize/ 1888." Included is the winner's name. The manufacturer's mark is stamped on the inside of the left leg. (This identical figure with a plain holder is marked number 161 in the 1886–87 Meriden Britannia catalog.) Grade C, $200 – 350.

Plate 650 & 651

Top and bottom: *Maker and number not marked. (Located: Wilcox Silver Plate Co., Number 01577.)* A young boy pulls a wheeled ring. Scrolls run from the axle to the shaft of the cart. This figure is occasionally found with a leaf under the boy's feet. *(See photo above.)* Both versions are correct. The support may have been found to be unnecessary for balance and discontinued or simply eliminated as a cost-cutting move. This figure was also used by several other makers.) Grade A, $500 and up.

Plate 652

Maker and number not marked. A barefoot boy pulls a napkin holder on wheels. The fancy, Victorian fretwork, which runs from the axle and supports the shaft, is a variation of the Wilcox Silver Plate Co, number 01577. Grade A, $500 and up.

Plate 653

Wilcox Silver Plate Co., Number 01576. A boy pulls a sled by a rope. The highly embossed napkin holder has an appliquéd banner for a monogram. An embossed bird with a leafy branch decorates the sides of the sled. Grade A, $500 and up.

Plate 654

Wm. Rogers Mfg. Co., Number 15. A young boy holding a rope is seated on a flower while leaning against the napkin holder which is elevated by a small, floral pedestal. The rectangular base is decorated with an acanthus leaf border. Grade C+, $200 – 350.

Plate 655

Maker and number not marked. A very small boy pulls on his boot, while seated on a stool. Grade C, $200 – 350.

Plate 656

Reed & Barton, Number 1266. A young, barefoot boy pushes with one hand against the napkin holder. Flower buds climb up its side. The napkin holder and boy are mounted on an oval base. Grade C+, $200 – 350.

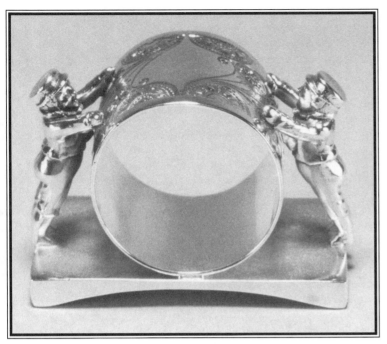

Plate 657

Middletown Plate Co., Number 87. Two small boys wearing caps lean against an embossed napkin holder mounted on a plain, rectangular base that has arched sides. Grade C, $200 – 350.

Plate 658

Wm. Rogers Mfg. Co., Number 19. A young boy holding a cookie plays with a frisky, crouching dog. The rectangular base with an acanthus leaf border is elevated by ball feet. (The napkin ring in plate 660 has the identical maker's mark and number, but there is no satisfactory explanation for this duplication.) Grade B, $350 – 500.

Plate 659

Derby Silver Co., Number 341. A young boy pulls off a sock while seated alongside the napkin holder. The other sock and his shoes rest by his feet. A ball is located behind the child. (The sock and shoes are often missing.) Grade C+, $200 – 350.

Plate 660

Wm. Rogers Mfg. Co., Number 19. A barefoot boy wearing short pants with suspenders and with hands in his pockets stands on a rectangular, tiered base. This figure resembles a Tom Sawyer type. A small bird with open wings perches on top of the napkin holder. (The napkin ring in Plate 658 has the identical maker's mark and number, but there is no satisfactory explanation for this duplication.) Grade B, $350 – 500.

Plate 661

Barbour Silver Co., Number 8. A young, barefoot boy, who resembles a Tom Sawyer type, stands with his hands in his pockets. The rectangular base is decorated with an acanthus leaf border. Grade B, $350 – 500.

Plate 662

Derby Silver Co., Number 328. A small boy wearing trousers with torn knees pulls a barrel-shaped napkin holder on a wheelbarrow base. Grade B, $350 – 500.

Plate 663

Maker and number not marked. A Tom Sawyer-type boy with his hands in his pockets stands in front of a napkin holder decorated with a rope edge. Grade C+, $200 – 350.

Plate 664

Toronto Silver Plate Co., Number 1148. A young boy wearing coattails and a shirt with ruffled front holds a hat in his left hand as he prepares to bow. The napkin holder is supported by a pair of short pedestals. The rectangular base, which is decorated with a zigzag border, is elevated by four raised feet. (The Toronto catalog shows the figure facing in the opposite direction.) Grade B, $350 – 500.

Plate 665

Maker not marked, Number 345. (Located: Derby Silver Co.) A small boy wearing trousers with torn knees pulls a napkin holder in the shape of a valise, which is mounted on a two-wheeled cart. A scroll extends from the rear of the cart. Grade A, $500 and up.

Plate 666

Left: *Meriden Britannia Co., Number 308.* A very small boy leaps over a fence alongside a napkin holder, mounted on a rectangular, ball-footed base. Grade C, $200 – 350. **Center:** *Meriden Britannia Co., Number 332.* Two very small boys suspended by palm fronds support a square napkin holder with open scrollwork border. Grade C, $200 – 350. **Right:** *Middletown Plate Co., Number 28.* See next photograph and caption.

Plate 667

Middletown Plate Co., Number 28. Two very small boys carry a napkin holder on their backs. The napkin holder is decorated with Japonaiserie design of bamboo and flowers and has an appliquéd shield for engraving. The rectangular base has an acanthus leaf border. (Note: Middletown produced this ring using different styles of napkin holders but with the same number.) Grade C, $200 – 350.

Plate 669

Aurora Silver Plate Co., Number 29. This true-to-life subject shows a young boy offering a begging dog a treat. The napkin holder is elevated by a pedestal. The irregular, octagonal base has a decorative design running around the border. Grade C+, $200 – 350.

Plate 668

Meriden Britannia Co., Number 199. A young boy makes his dog sit up for a tidbit, which is held in his left hand. Small, Victorian boys were often dressed in skirts. The plain base is flat and rectangular. Grade C+, $200 – 350.

Plate 670

Maker not marked, Number 10. (Located: Wm. Rogers Mfg. Co.) A young boy wearing a vest and skirt stands on a triple-tiered, oval base. (This boy is found on many silver-plated items, such as toothpick holders and card receivers.) Grade C, $200 – 350.

Plate 671

Maker not marked, Number 0254. (Located: Meriden Silver Plate Co.) A young boy dressed in a coat and cap hawks newspapers. (This is a well detailed figure.) Grade C+, $200 – 350.

Plate 672

Middletown Plate Co., Number 340. A pair of heralds holding clarions are mounted on each side of the napkin holder. A tiny, child's ring, the holder measures 1⁷⁄₁₆" in diameter and rests on a plain rectangular base, just 2⅛" long by 1¹⁄₁₆" wide. Grade D, under $200.

Plate 673

Reed & Barton, Number 1346. A young sailor boy ties an anchor around the napkin holder with a rope. Six leaf legs decorate and elevate the rectangular base. Grade B+, $350 – 500.

Plate 674

Simpson, Hall, Miller & Co., Number 06. A sailor boy and an anchor with a rope support the napkin holder on a rectangular base with chamfered corners. Grade B+, $350 – 500.

Plate 675

Simpson, Hall, Miller & Co., Number 06. This is a front view of the previous napkin ring. Grade B+, $350 – 500.

Plate 676

Left: *Derby Silver Co., Number 379.* A baby boy, who is lying on his stomach with legs crossed in the air, features a bare derriere. He balances the napkin holder on his head and feet. Grade C, $200 – 350. **Right:** *Meriden Britannia Co., Number 159.* A child dressed in shorts stands on a ball mounted on a round base. His arms are raised with a drumstick in each hand. He supports the napkin holder, designed as a drum, by a rope around his neck. Grade C+, $200 – 350.

Plate 677

Maker and number not marked. A boy scout holding a staff salutes as he stands by the napkin holder. (Rumor has it that the staff held an American flag. However, this cannot be verified. No break-points or solder marks can be found on the staffs that have been examined.) Grade B, $350 – 500.

Girls

Plate 678

Meriden Britannia Co., Number 280. A smiling, sweet, little girl with her hair in a long braid, wears an apron. She pushes the napkin holder. Grade C, $200 – 350.

Plate 679

Southington Silver Plate Co., Number not marked. A smiling, little girl with her hair in a long braid wears an apron. She pushes a napkin holder, which is decorated with flowers, leaves, and berries. (This rectangular base with a fluted border was used by this manufacturer with various other figures. The above figure was also utilized by Meriden Britannia Co. after it acquired Southington in the early 1890s.) Grade C+, $200 – 350.

Plate 680

Middletown Plate Co., Number 107. A young girl with her hair in a ponytail carries a single flower in her left hand and a basket of flowers in her right. Overlapping leaves form the base upon which she stands. Grade C+, $200 – 350.

Plate 681

Left: *Meriden Britannia Co., Number 330.* A smiling, sweet, little girl skips a rope in front of the napkin holder, which is suspended from her skirt. The plain oval base is elevated by four ball feet. Skipping rope was a favorite pastime of Victorian children as it is today. Grade B+, $350 – 500. **Right:** *Wilcox Silver Plate Co., Number 01548.* An oval shield base decorated with stars and stripes holds a girl lying on her stomach. She supports a scalloped-edged napkin holder. Grade B, $350 – 500.

Plate 682

Derby Silver Co., Number 319. A young girl with her hair tied by a ribbon holds a bouquet of flowers. The napkin holder with cutouts on its edges has a cinched-in center. The large, oval base with decorative feet adds height and importance to this ring. (The maker's mark is in large, raised, capital letters on the underside of this base.) Grade C+, $200 – 350.

Plate 684

Maker not marked, Number 0262 (Located: Meriden Silver Plate Co.) A young girl immersed in reading a book sits on a snail in front of the napkin holder. Is she a slow reader? Grade C+, $200 – 350.

Plate 683

Maker and number not marked. A crying child sits astride a plain napkin holder mounted on a raised, circular pedestal. Grade C, $200 – 350.

Plate 685

Toronto Silver Plate Co., Number 1147. A large girl (3⅜" high) wears an early 1800s attire. She has a muff pushed up on her left arm. The napkin holder is elevated by a short pedestal and mounted on a footed, rectangular base. (The figure is attached to the base by two bolts and nuts.) Grade B, $350 – 500.

Plate 686

Derby Silver Co., Number 306. A girl holding a bas
ket is seated on a bell-shaped flower. An undulat
ing stem extends to form a handle, which ends in a
leaf. Other unique features of this napkin ring are
the arched napkin holder and elaborate, rectangu
lar base. (Also found marked Wm. Rogers & Son
number 16.) Grade B+, $350 – 500.

Men

Plate 687

*Maker and number not marked. (Located: Barbour
Silver Co., Number 2904.)* Sometimes referred to
by collectors as the "Dapper Young Man," he
wears a waistcoat, which shows below his cut-away
coat, neckwear tied in a bow, knee breeches, and a
top hat. This attire was popular circa 1800. The
napkin holder with an overall raised design has
fluted borders. (A mate to this napkin ring features
a young lady with the identical napkin holder.)
Grade B+, $350 – 500.

Plate 688

Southington Cutlery Co., Number 41. A pair of busts of Greco-Roman men balance a napkin holder on their heads. The square base has a fluted border. Grade C, $200 – 350.

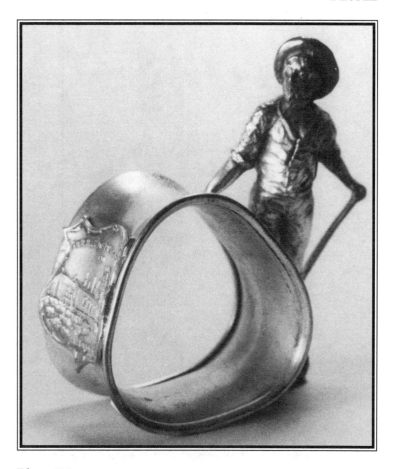

Plate 689

Maker and number not marked. This souvenir napkin holder reads "Summit of Pike's Peak, Col./ Alt. 14,147 ft." A gold miner stands on a rock and holds a pickax alongside the triangular napkin holder. The cast, appliquéd shield shows a monument and the inscription. Grade C, $200 – 350.

Plate 690

Rogers & Brother, Number not marked. A gold miner standing on a rocky mound holds a pickax on a plain, round, elevated base. His thigh and hand are attached to a decorated napkin holder. This nicely detailed figure is one of a few with an early Western theme. Grade C+, $200 – 350.

Plate 691

Van Bergh Silver Plate Co., Number 144. A gold miner stands on a rock and holds a pickax. The plain base is raised and round. Grade C+, $200 – 350.

Plate 692

Derby Silver Co., Number 383. A European dandy wearing a cutaway coat and a bicorne (cocked) hat leans on a napkin holder, which has raised bands. (Something is missing from his right hand, possibly a walking stick, baton or riding crop.) Grade C, $200 – 350.

Plate 693

Maker not marked, Number 67. (Possibly Aurora Silver Plate Co.) An Oriental man holds a heavy bamboo pole. A rope connects the pole to a square napkin holder that rests on a round base decorated with woodland flora. Grade B, $350 – 500.

Plate 694

Left: *Simpson, Hall, Miller & Co., Number 023.* A workman carries a barrel-shaped napkin holder on his back. The rectangular base with chamfered corners simulates mounded earth. Grade B, $350 – 500.

Right: *Maker not marked, Number 1145. (Located: Reed & Barton.)* A bearded workman on bended knee lifts a napkin holder above his head. (Some collectors label this napkin ring "Atlas," which is wishful thinking to give it higher value. A close examination shows that he is an ordinary workman.) Grade C+, $200 – 350.

Plate 695

James W. Tufts, Number 1516. A baker holds a vertical napkin holder, which has the shape of a flour barrel. (One might assume that this is a toothpick holder with a missing base; however, Tufts produced an identical baker carrying a toothpick holder, number 2642.) Grade B, $350 – 500.

1508. Per dozen, $36.00.
Gold and Oxidized, per dozen, 54.00.

Plate 696

Reed & Barton, Number 1508. A kneeling Egyptian man holds a napkin holder by a rod with ball ends. The holder is decorated with buds and flowers of the lotus, which occur in ancient Egyptian ornamentation. Grade C+, $200 – 350.

Plate 697

This is an illustration from the 1885 Reed & Barton catalog.

Plate 698

Meriden Silver Plate Co., Number 220. An Eskimo, standing on a section of ice, holds an ice cutter. The napkin holder with wide decorated borders is mounted on a plain, raised, round base. (An ice blade—a long triangular wedge—is missing off the bottom of the handle and the top of the handle has been broken off this example.) Grade C+, $200 – 350.

Plate 699

Maker and number not marked. This electroplated nickel silver (EPNS) piece has an Australian subject. A native standing on a log base prepares to throw a boomerang. He wears only a loin cloth. Grade D, under $200.

Plate 700

Maker and number not marked. A bust of Abraham Lincoln has the name "Lincoln" stamped at its base. The napkin holder is elevated by a ball pedestal on an openwork, oval base. (It is unusual to find a napkin ring of a public figure, such as Lincoln.) Grade C, $200 – 350.

Women

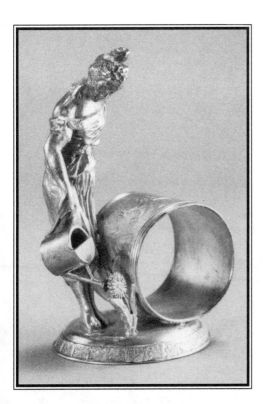

Plate 701

Meriden Silver Plate Co., Number 0229. A graceful, slender, and beautiful lady with bare feet holds a watering can. Below it is one flower. The round base has a raised, decorated border. Grade B+, $350 – 500.

Plate 702

W.R., Number 340. (Wm. A. Rogers, Ltd.) A lady's head, wearing what is probably a nurse's cap, rests atop a napkin holder on a raised, round base with a decorated border. Grade C, $200 – 350.

Plate 703

Southington Cutlery Co., Number 42. The head of a Victorian lady wearing a hat balances an attractive napkin holder on her head. Grade C, $200 – 350.

Plate 704

Maker and number not marked. (Located: Barbour Silver Co., Number 2903.) A smart looking young lady with arms akimbo stands in front of a napkin holder with scalloped edges. She wears clothing typical of circa 1800. (This napkin ring is a mate to the dapper young man, Barbour, number 2904.) Grade B+, $350 – 500.

Plate 705

Wilcox Silver Plate Co., Number 01556. A seated woman with cloth draped over the lower body and wearing a necklace sits with crossed legs on a large, unusual, lyre-shaped base, which is elevated by ball feet. The napkin holder, with flared ends, has a center band embossed with birds and flowers. Grade B, $350 – 500.

Plate 706

Reed & Barton, Number 1175. A frisky, barking dog follows a young woman in Victorian dress. She carries the napkin holder by tasseled cords. The small, oval, elevated base has a textured upper surface and polished border. (This napkin ring is illustrated in an 1877 Reed & Barton catalog.) Grade B, $350 – 500.

Plate 707

Aurora Silver Plate Co., Number 45. A young woman, dressed in a coat and hat, carries a purse and walks alongside a napkin holder elevated on a short pedestal. The flat, rectangular base has chamfered corners. Grade B, $350 – 500.

Plate 708

Wm. Rogers Mfg. Co., Number 10. A barefoot woman wearing a head kerchief and apron stands with arms akimbo on a tiered, oval base strewn with field flowers on its upper surface. Grade B, $350 – 500.

Plate 709

Southington Cutlery Co., Number 39. A lady in elegant attire, complete with hat, shawl, and a gown with a bustle, stands holding a spyglass against the napkin holder. The style of her dress is 1875, high fashion for this era. Grade C+, $200 – 350.

While the more popular sports of tennis, golf, baseball, and tobogganing are represented in figural napkin rings, they are still few and far between. Today, napkin rings with a tennis or baseball theme are popular collectibles. Many fakes and reproductions are appearing on the market, although this has not lessened the desire of experienced collectors to own the originals.

Plate 710

Left: *Meriden Britannia Co., Number 284.* A male tennis player, who holds a court tennis racket, wears early 1900s sports clothes and stands beside a napkin holder with a scalloped and beaded edge. (No authentic tennis player on a base has been documented to date.) Grade A+, $500 and up. **Right:** *Rogers, Smith & Co., Number 283.* A female tennis player, who holds a court tennis racket, wears a turn-of-the-century dress and stands next to an identical napkin holder as the male. (The manufacturer's mark on the base of her skirt is on a coin. Rogers, Smith & Co. was absorbed by Meriden Britannia Co. Later pieces will have the same number with Meriden's name.) Grade A+, $500 and up.

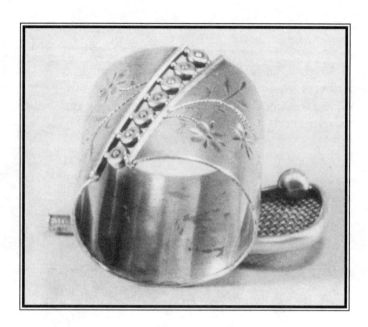

Plate 711

Meriden Britannia Co., Number 310. A cutout design on the top of the napkin holder gives it special character. A tennis racket with a tennis ball serves as the base. Grade C, $200 – 350.

Plate 712

Stix and L'Allemand, Number 55. Three crossed tennis rackets, which elevate a barrel-shaped napkin holder, rest on a round base that also holds three tennis balls. A series of anthemions are embossed in the base's border. (This New York company was probably a jobber or jeweler. Grade B, $350 – 500.

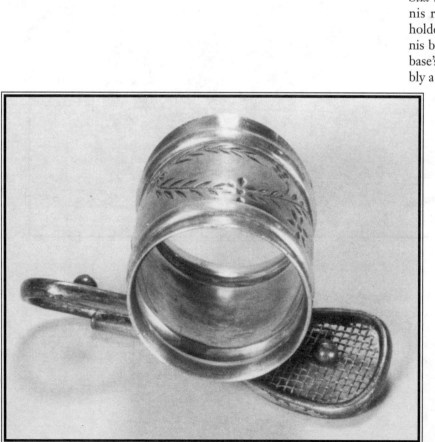

Plate 713

M B CO., Number 310. (Meriden Britannia Co.) A pair of matching tennis rackets with tennis balls centered on the strings serves as the base of the napkin holder. Engraved leaves and flowers decorate the center of the napkin holder. (The maker's mark and number are located on one handle.) Grade C+ $200 – 350.

Plate 714

Reed & Barton, Number 1455. A lady in a pretty, long dress with ruffled hem holds a badminton racket in her right hand and a shuttlecock in her left. She stands on a plain, flat, rectangular base. Grade B+, $350 – 500.

Plate 715

Meriden Britannia Co., Number 658. A pair of table tennis paddles are surrounded by laurel leaves, symbolizing victory. A scroll handle is fastened to the napkin holder, which has an openwork border. The plain oval base is elevated by four ball feet. Grade B, $350 – 500.

Plate 716

Adelphi Silver Plate Co., Number 11. A draped child, who rides a high wheeled bicycle, holds a small victory wreath. A pair of scrolls supports the napkin holder. (Caution: A recent spate of reproductions of this ring has appeared.) Grade A, $500 and up.

Plate 717

Meriden Britannia Co., Number 647. The handles of a pair of brooms cross through a round, victory wreath. A curling stone lies in front. Curling is a sport played on ice, popular in Canada. Grade C+, $200 – 350.

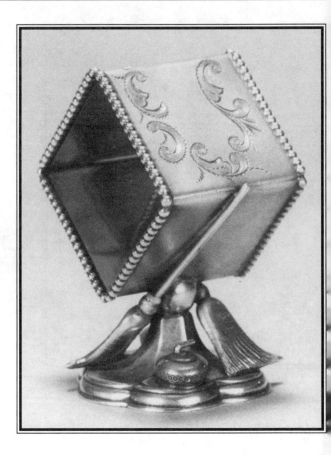

Plate 718

Meriden Britannia Co., Number 684. Crossed brooms and the stone for the game of curling are set on a scalloped-border base. (Originating in Scotland, the game uses brooms to send stones spinning over ice to a target circle. The game is also popular in Canada, America, and other countries where there is ice.) Grade C+, $200 – 350.

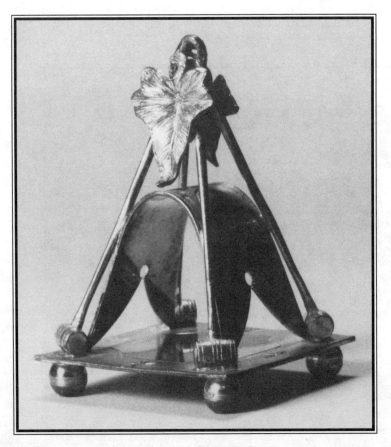

Plate 719

Derby Silver Co., Number 302. Four croquet mallets are artfully joined at the top with flowers. The chased napkin holder simulates a wicket. The square base has ball feet. Grade C+, $200 – 350.

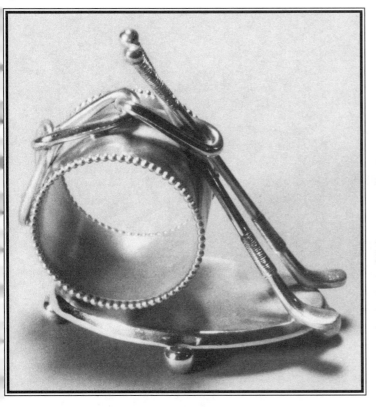

Plate 721

Plate 720

Meriden Britannia Co., Number 656. Early golf clubs rest against a very large napkin holder (2⅛" in diameter) and are held by chain links draped over the holder. This item is a play on the words "golf links." Grade C+, $200 – 350.

Derby Silver Co., Number 336. A pair of horseshoes form the napkin holder, which is topped by a jockey cap. The rectangular, tiered base is decorated on the top with woodland flora. Grade C+, $200 – 350.

Plate 722

Pairpoint Manufacturing Co., Number 83. A baseball player, dressed in a turn-of-the-century uniform, prepares to throw the ball held in his right hand. A bat and glove lie on the square base, which simulates an earthen surface. Grade A+, $500 and up.

Plate 723

Meriden Britannia Co., Number 249. A man, dressed in sports attire, stands alongside a napkin holder elevated on a pedestal. His outfit dates in the 1880s. Grade B, $350 – 500.

Plate 724

Maker not marked, Number 035. (Located: Simpson, Hall, Miller & Co.) A Kate Greenaway-type boy stands with hands behind his back and holds a baseball bat. The ball is located by his right foot. (This ring is sought after by both Greenaway collectors and baseball fans.) Grade B+, $350 – 500.

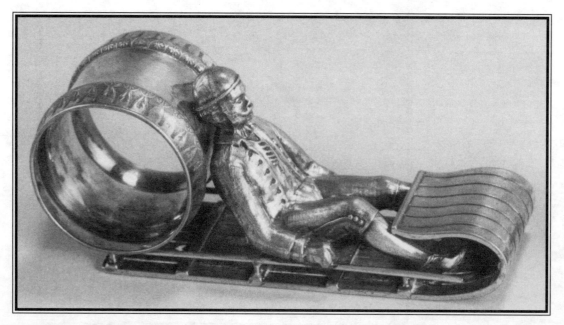

Plate 725

Wilcox Silver Plate Co., Number 4343. A man dressed in sports attire leans back against the napkin holder as he sits on a toboggan. He grips the handrails as if in a racing position. Grade A+, $500 and up.

Plate 726

James W. Tufts, Number 1655. A Kate Greenaway-type boy wearing a tasseled hat rides on a toboggan. The napkin holder rests on the sled's side supports. Grade A+, $500 and up.

Plate 727

James W. Tufts, Number 1655. This closeup of the above napkin holder shows the head of a hunting dog with a game bird in its mouth.

Plate 728

Wilcox Silver Plate Co., Number 4342. A Kate Greenaway-type lady in a long dress and wearing a showy big hat sits on a toboggan and supports the napkin holder in her lap. (This is a beautiful napkin ring despite an incongruous combination of lovely summer clothes and a winter sport.) Grade A+, $500 and up.

Plate 729

West Silver Co., Number 273. A seated woman dressed in heavy clothing and wearing a hood rides a toboggan while grasping the decorated napkin holder. (This ring was also produced, marked F. B. Rogers Silver Co. with the same number.) Grade B+, $350 – 500.

Plate 730

Meriden Silver Plate Co., Number 288. A pair of swords in sheaths and hunting horns supports a napkin holder. Underneath the holder and centered on the oval base is a riding cap. The raised border of the base is decorated with acanthus leaves and small flowers. Grade C+, $200 – 350.

Plate 731

Maker not marked, Number 86 or 98. The handle of a tennis racket leans against a tennis ball, which connects to a plain napkin holder. A short tree branch adds support and balance at the base. Grade C+, $200 – 350.

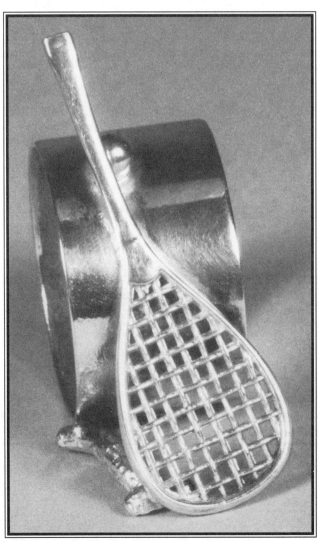

FAKES, MISTAKES AND MYSTERIES

In this chapter, fakes, mistakes, and mysteries are defined as follows: **FAKE:** *A napkin ring that has been fabricated or altered in an attempt to pass it off as authentic; a counterfeit or forgery.* **MISTAKE:** *A napkin ring that has missing or broken parts or has incorrect parts.* **MYSTERY:** *A napkin ring that has some element that is unexplained and, therefore, questionable.*

It should be made clear that several objects in this chapter are good, old, original items with only missing or broken parts. A few are married, that is, joined with other old, original parts, but an incorrect combination.

Detecting reproductions is obviously made easier when the napkin ring can be compared and studied alongside documented authentic old pieces. Differences in details, plating (if present), patina, and material can be studied. Fake napkin rings may sometimes be detected by the presence of spin marks inside the napkin holders. Another hint may be a prominent seam mark on the napkin holder. (A seam mark on the holder should not be confused with a line used for decoration.)

Unfortunately, the best teachers are mistakes. Even the most experienced collectors and dealers will admit that they have made them. A good education can come from the crankiest dealers, once they know that you are serious. Reliable dealers will issue written guarantees of authenticity with return privileges (with time limits). Most dealers who specialize in figural napkin rings have already made their mistakes, and by the time hundreds of rings have passed through their hands, they should be able to spot a reproduction.

Novices should attempt to learn everything possible about figural napkin rings. They should study catalogs and books, learn the importance of manufacturers' identification numbers, view pieces at auctions and antiques shows, and make friends with dealers and collectors who will be willing to guide them. The most powerful tool necessary for purchasing figural napkin rings is knowledge. It pays to take time to learn the field in order to protect your investment.

Sometimes it is merely a desire to want the napkin ring to be real that makes an individual fall for it. If the napkin ring is priced too cheaply, then it is important to take another look.

The numbering systems of most manufacturers give clues to some forgeries and marriages. For example, perfume stands and toothpick holders have had their bottles and toothpick holders removed and replaced with napkin holders. The forger most likely made use of a piece with a missing glass bottle. A few of these made-up napkin rings are shown in this book as examples.

Over 20 years have passed since *American Victorian Figural Napkin Rings* was published. Even then, the author Victor Schnadig warned of reproductions and what he termed "homemade figurals," those pieces made from married parts. Reproductions in the 1960s from Japan were new, unmarked (except for paper labels), and easy to spot. However, in this high-tech age of the 90s, reproductions and forgeries are skillfully made to purposely fool a buyer. Furthermore, they are being manufactured right here in the U.S.A. as well as overseas. Time and care are given to these fakes for the simple reason that it pays well. Recent high interest and competition for the original, old tabletop jewels have sent prices skyrocketing. While Schnadig felt secure in his selections in the 60s because "they are marked," reproductions are now found with manufacturers' marks and some numbers are correct.

Some authentic and important figural napkin rings carry no manufacturers' marks or numbers. Some carry one or the other.

Collectors-dealers Ron and Joyce Bronow discovered that James W. Tufts' napkin ring numbers range from 1400 to 1699 only. Unfortunately, Tufts was the only manufacturer to use consecutive numbers for napkin rings within a restricted range. The numbers of other companies followed a variety of patterns. For example, Meriden Britannia Co. limited napkin ring numbers to 100s, 200s, and 300s. Their combination sets are two digits. Napkin rings with numbers in the 600s, produced by Meriden Britannia Co., are from its Canadian branch. Pairpoint Manufacturing Co. marked napkin rings with one or two digit numbers, and their combination sets were marked in the 200s. Many of the numbers of the Wilcox Silver Plate Co. were five digits started with a zero, but they used other numbers as well.

Fakes

Plate 732

James W. Tufts, Number 3405. Unfortunately, this beautiful napkin ring is a fake. The Kate Greenaway-type lady wearing a large, showy hat stands by a napkin holder elevated on a pedestal. This number in the Tufts' 1880s catalog reveals a toothpick holder with an art-glass insert where the napkin holder has been placed in this example. See adjacent catalog illustration.

Plate 733

James W. Tufts, Number 3405. This is an illustration from the Tufts' 1880s catalog.

Plate 734

Derby Silver Co., Number 3520. This magnificent and large figural piece (5¼" by 3¾") could easily pass as an authentic napkin ring. However, the clue that this is a fake is the number, which in the catalog reveals an elaborate card receiver. See adjacent catalog illustration.

Plate 735

This illustration from the Derby's 1883 catalog proves the point.

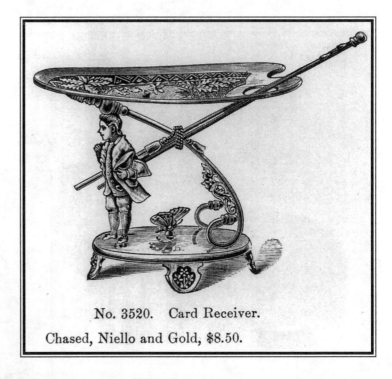

No. 3520. Card Receiver.

Chased, Niello and Gold, $8.50.

Plate 736

James W. Tufts, Number 1161. This lady with an elaborate hat is a perfect example of an altered piece, most likely done for monetary gain. The pedestal, here supporting a napkin holder, was originally a very ornate vase holder, which included a large glass vase. See adjacent catalog illustration.

Plate 737

James W. Tufts, Number 1161. The proper arrangement is shown in Tuft's 1880s catalog.

Plate 738

Meriden Silver Plate Co., Number 252. Every part of this napkin ring is original except the Brownies. These have been added and are most likely taken from a knife rest. (See the correct napkin ring in the Miscellaneous Subjects chapter.)

Plate 739

Simpson, Hall, Miller & Co., Number not marked. Signs of alterations on this item include irregular cuts on the carriage section and uneven solder, thus condemning this elegant looking wheeled object as a forgery. The carriage section was produced as a perfume holder. See adjacent photograph.

Plate 740

This photograph shows the correct combination.

Plate 741

James W. Tufts, Number 2081. The number on the base of this item is shown in the Tufts' catalog as the bottom half of a spoon holder. The lady swimmer and napkin holder are additions. See adjacent catalog illustration.

AS SHOWN GOLD-LINED, $3.50
PLAIN WITHOUT GOLD, 3.00

Plate 742

James W. Tufts, Number 2081. This illustration from Tufts' 1880s catalog shows that only the pedestal of this spoon holder was used to produce the fake napkin ring.

Plate 743

Meriden Britannia Co., Number 219. A close examination discloses a clever use of parts. The base, originally from a bud-vase napkin ring, has been married with the upper parts of a call bell. (See correct napkin ring in Chapter 4.)

Plate 744

James W. Tufts, Number 3069. The above number is a perfume stand and is illustrated in the Tufts' 1880s catalog. See adjacent catalog illustration.

Plate 745

James W. Tufts, Number 3069. This is the illustration taken from Tufts' 1880s catalog.

Plate 746

Meriden Britannia Co., Number 411. Based on the number, this piece is questionable as a napkin ring. No Meriden Britannia napkin rings have been located in the catalogs in the 400 numbers; these numbers identify vase holders.

Plate 747

Pairpoint Manufacturing Co., Number 3705. This piece is a fake. The Pairpoint catalog shows that Number 3705 is a bear with a toothpick holder on the base that is shown here. The Oriental figure and napkin holder have been married to this base.

Plate 748

Maker and number not marked. A large ear of corn stands by a souvenir napkin holder with raised decorations of "Leselle Gymnasium," "Morgan Hall," and "Thompson Laboratories." Close inspection reveals the corn to be a salt shaker; the holes are plugged with silver solder. Globs of solder fasten the napkin holder and obscure part of the souvenir design.

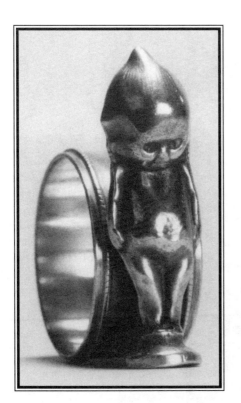

Plate 749

Maker and number not marked. This Kewpie figure is too recent to be a product of the Victorian period. The Rose O'Neill Kewpies (winged cupids) first appeared in the year 1912. Close examination shows that this figure is cast of a soft lead-like material.

Plate 750

James W. Tufts, Number 3072. Although a perfect example of a napkin ring that looks authentic, the napkin holder is a replacement for a perfume bottle. The Tufts' catalog shows the boy holding a cut-glass perfume bottle in his arms. Also missing is a tall stemmed flower, which is anchored to one end of the base. See adjacent catalog illustration.

3072 Silver, $3.75
Silver & Gold, 4.25

Plate 751

James W. Tufts, Number 3072. This is an illustration from the Tufts's 1880s catalog.

Plate 752

Left: *Maker not marked, Number 035. (Located: Simpson, Hall, Miller & Co.)* This napkin ring is a fine, old original and is illustrated here for comparison with the forgery on the right. **Right:** *Maker and number not marked.* A reproduced Kate Greenaway-type boy with baseball and bat has one tell-tale and obvious clue, which is the seam line joining the napkin holder. This line is not be confused with decorative lines found on authentic napkin holders.

Plate 753

James W. Tufts, Number 2648. This napkin ring looks perfect in every way, but an 1880s Tufts' catalog revealed its secret: it is a fake. A napkin holder replaced the original rod spanning the workman's shoulders, which held a pair of swinging toothpick holders. See adjacent catalog illustration.

Plate 754

James W. Tufts, Number 2648. This is an illustration from the Tufts' 1880s catalog.

Plate 755

Wm. Rogers Mfg. Co., Number not marked. If original, this piece would be marvelous, but, unfortunately, it is a fake. This piece has surfaced in many numbers in recent years. The maker's mark on a coin proves that the forgers even reproduced the coins.

Plate 756

Simpson, Hall, Miller & Co., Number not marked.. When Palmer Cox Brownie figures are found on napkin rings, extra special caution should be taken for assurance that they are authentic pieces. The original figures are relatively scarce on napkin rings. Examination of this ring leads to the conclusion that it is a modern-day product. In other words, a fake. The figures are without detail, and they don't have the proper patina.

Plate 757

Maker and number not marked. A view of a hollow casting found on one example of a reproduction of a Greenaway-type boy. This particular piece along with the matching girl—if authentic—is closed on the base, where the maker's mark and number are found. These Greenaway reproductions, which were unmarked except for paper labels, were imported from Japan in large numbers in the late 1960s. They sold for $20.00 for the pair retail.

Plate 758

Meriden Britannia Co., Number 30. Jack and the Beanstalk, while looking good and authentic, is not located in Meriden's catalog nor is the number 30 found in Meriden's order of numbers for napkin rings.

Plate 759

Meriden Silver Plate Co., Number 1024. The above number is shown in the manufacturer's 1879 catalog as a card receiver. This piece has been altered with the addition of the large bird and a napkin holder. See adjacent catalog illustration.

Plate 760

Meriden Silver Plate Co., Number 1024. This is an illustration from the 1879 Meriden Silver Plate Co. catalog.

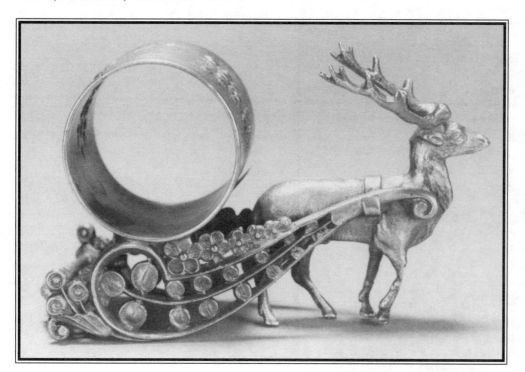

Plate 761

Toronto Silver Plate Co., Number not marked. This is a sensational looking ring; however, it is a reproduction. The mark is on a coin. While this is a skillful copy, the traits of a reproduction are evident. Cast from a heavy metal, it lacks the fine details of an original piece, which is apparent to the educated eye. The holder is exceptionally crude and has been found on several different reproduced napkin rings.

Plate 762

Derby Silver Co., Number 828. Number 828 indicates a caster set by this maker in its 1883 catalog. Derby did not repeat numbers. This is a skillful casting; only a study of the company's catalog numbers proves it is a forgery.

Plate 763

James W. Tufts, Number 2200. This ring is a reproduced combination of figures and base taken from Tufts' inventory; however, the forger used a number that was not employed by Tufts for napkin rings. Tufts' numbers for napkin rings begin at 1400 and end with 1699. (This reproduced item may have the maker's mark without a number.)

Plate 764

Pairpoint Manufacturing Co., Number 5604. This number shown in the Pairpoint catalog proves that this item is a combination thermometer and ring tree. The napkin holder has been soldered onto the base of what was the ring tree, and the backdrop holding the thermometer has been cut off. See adjacent photograph.

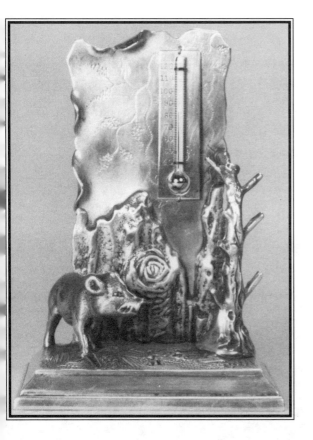

Plate 765

Pairpoint Manufacturing Co. Number 5604. This photograph shows the correct object for this number.

Plate 766

Reed & Barton, Number 3074. The giraffe and palm tree in this cake stand have been removed and recast for use in faked napkin rings. This style palm tree has never been incorporated in authentic napkin rings. This tree paired with a camel has also been seen, although it is a combination that was never made as a legitimate napkin ring.

Plate 767

Stewart & Jones, Number not marked. This napkin ring is an altered piece with missing parts. The figure of a girl stands where a pepper shaker or salt cellar should be anchored on a peg. Parts have been cut off that held other accessories for what was originally a combination set. (Rogers, Smith & Co. produced this combination set with number 21. Stewart & Jones were probably retailers.)

Mistakes

Plate 768

James W. Tufts, Number 1456. A Kate Greenaway-type girl wearing a bonnet with a scarf stands with her back to a fancy, cutout napkin holder on a base with three feet. The problem is the missing pepper shaker and open salt dish, which were anchored by pegs and located on either corner in front of the girl. The pegs were probably ground off when the pair of condiments were lost. (Suspicion should be aroused when the base is too large for the component parts.)

Plate 769

Rogers, Smith & Co., Number 21. The butter plate is a substitute on this combination set, and the salt and pepper containers differ from an illustration in the manufacturer's catalog. Loose condiment parts were highly susceptible to loss and incorrect replacement. See adjacent catalog illustration.

No. 21. INDIVIDUAL CASTER $4.75
Salt, Pepper, Butter Plate and Napkin Ring.

Plate 770

This is an illustration from an unknown wholesale jobber's catalog.

Plate 771

Maker and number not marked. The salt and pepper set in the shape of pineapples is on an oak leaf base. The correct salt and pepper are shaped like acorns. This is a married piece.

Plate 772

Maker and number not marked. (Located: Derby Silver Co., Number 303.) This is an excellent example of a napkin ring with major parts missing. This object stresses the importance of study and research of catalogs even when no numbers are available. See adjacent catalog illustration.

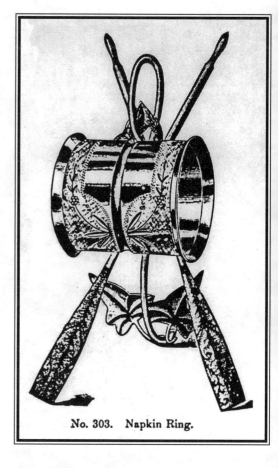

No. 303.   Napkin Ring.

Plate 773

Derby Silver Co., Number 303. This is an illustration from a Derby Silver Co. catalog.

Plate 775

Meriden Britannia Co., Number 657. This is an illustration from a Meriden Britannia Co. catalog.

Plate 774

Meriden Britannia Co., Number 657. A triangular napkin holder is draped with chain links and a pair of golf clubs whose handles are broken off. Collectors have mistakenly called these hockey sticks. See adjacent catalog illustration.

Plate 776

James W. Tufts, Number 1607. Shown here is an early, original napkin clip with a reclining Kate Greenaway-type boy. An 1880s Tufts' catalog reveals a large flower that decorates both sides of the napkin clip. This decoration is missing. Close examination will show the remaining solder on the clip's front edge. See adjacent catalog illustration.

Plate 777

James W. Tufts, Number 1607. This is an illustration from the Tufts' 1880s catalog.

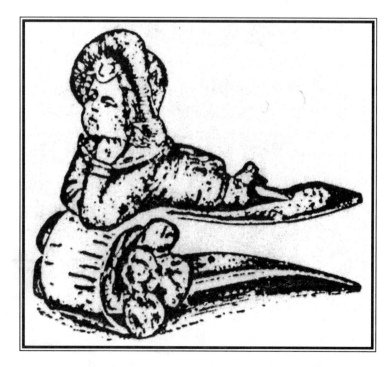

Plate 779

Toronto Silver Plate Co., Number 1701. This is an illustration from the 1888 catalog of the Toronto Silver Plate Co..

Plate 778

Hartford Silver Plate Co., Number 651. A standing, dressed fox on a raised, circular, pedestaled base is the major interest of this combination set. The butter plate and salt and pepper shakers are replacements, which considerably diminish its value. This combination set was also produced by Toronto Silver Plate Co., Number 1701. See adjacent catalog illustration.

Mysteries

Plate 780

Maker and number not marked. A golfer in knickers and kiltie-tie shoes appears to be a late production item—not Victorian—and possibly of limited production. There is a strong possibility that this napkin ring was made up to sell to golf enthusiasts.

Plate 782

This is a photograph of the Lime Kiln Club cigar-box label of 1883. Note the man on the far left, who is wearing an identical, Civil War cap as the man on the napkin ring.

Plate 781

Derby Silver Co., Number 5. At first glance, one would think this item quite improbable for a Victorian table. Yet as a Lime Kiln Club cigar-box label shows, caricatures of African-Americans were created in the 1880s. The possibility exists that this napkin ring was of a limited edition, produced for a club or a special purpose. See adjacent illustration.

Plate 783

Poole Silver Co., Number 122. This is a legitimate napkin ring, and is shown here because the object that this cherub held in its hands is missing and a mystery. Poole, not widely known for napkin rings, has used this base, which is typical of Middletown Plate Co. Catalogs from these two companies are scarce.

Plate 784

Wilcox Silver Plate Co., Number 01513. A large, draped, winged Cupid with a quiver of arrows on his back holds a bow in his right hand. The post that supports the napkin holder on one side has been seen with both a glass bud vase in a holder and a silver-plated bud vase mounted on it. In each case, they have been resoldered to the post, which is evidently a weak spot. This raises the question about the original design.

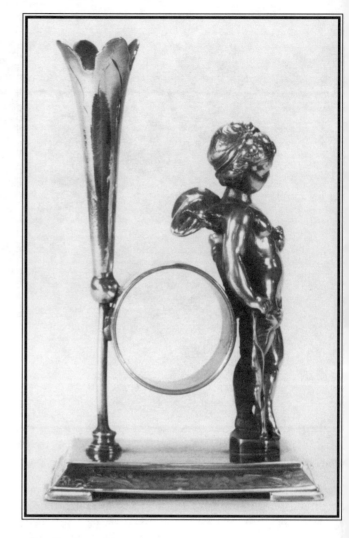

Plate 785

Manning, Bowman & Co., Number 01513. This is an example of the previous napkin ring with a bud vase that has been resoldered, raising a question as to its authenticity. Is the bud vase original to the napkin ring or a replacement? This problem arises when solder is so obviously poor and the search for a catalog illustration has been unsuccessful. If the design is correct, it is apparent that the joining of the bud vase has produced a weak spot. Judging from the number, the ring was most likely a Wilcox Silver Plate Co. product and marketed by Manning, Bowman.

Plate 786

Wilcox Silver Plate Co., Number 3614. A girl holding an easel is a unique piece designed to hold a menu or place card. There is no doubt that this is an authentic piece; however, there is a question of whether it is also a napkin ring where the napkin would be placed behind the easel. This object has been included in this chapter pending proof of its original purpose.

Plate 787

Reed & Barton, Number 276. This is an original and wonderful figural object, which is actually a toothpick holder but can easily accommodate a napkin in the open space between the mortar on carriage and the sailor boy. Whether or not this is a dual purpose item has yet to be determined.

Plate 788

Maker and number not marked. Some collectors have insisted that this napkin ring was never produced in the early days. In other words, only modern editions exist. Careful examination of this piece shows a finely detailed cat and cart. While no numbers are found on this item, this is not uncommon on wheeled carts. Although this particular piece is believed to be an original, it is relegated to this chapter because of the doubts still held by a majority of experts who have yet to examine it. True, all the other cat carts that have been examined to date are reproductions.

Plate 789

Meriden Britannia Co., Number not marked. This is a boy with a staff on which there is an elevated napkin holder. Elevated holders are unusual, but plenty of examples exist. There is a serious question as to the authenticity of this napkin ring.

No. 62732. Napkin Ring, fancy, with raised ornamentation. Price, 75c.

No. 62733. Napkin Ring, with bird on wish-bone, fancy. Price, 90c.

No. 62734. Napkin Ring on lily, satin finished, fancy. Price, $1.05.

No. 62737. Tooth Pick or Match Holder, gold lined, bright burnished, with fancy raised ornamentation. Price, 60c.

No. 62738. Tooth Pick or Match Holder, gold lined, bright burnished, with very fancy raised ornamentation. Price, $1.05.

No. 62739. Tooth Pick Holder, gold lined, satin finished, with fancy ornamentation. Price, $1.35.

No. 62740. Tooth Pick Holder, gold lined, satin finished, with fancy ornamentation. Price, $1.35.

Plate 790

An illustration from an 1897 Sears, Roebuck & Co. catalog.

Plate 791

An illustration from an 1897 Sears, Roebuck & Co. catalog with special information on the monkey band napkin rings. Note: The bottom of the catalog page has written "We can furnish the 'Monkey Band' Napkin Ring in the following pieces, namely: The Leader, First Violin, Base Viol, Clarionet, Bassoon, Triangle, Cymbals, and a few others. We have bought the entire lot of these Rings and are selling them at about one-half real value."

No. 62735. Fancy Napkin Ring, satin finished and chased. Price, $1.30.

No. 62736. Fancy Napkin Ring, satin finished and chased. Price, $1.30.

No. 62741. "The Monkey Band" Napkin Ring, with very fancy raised ornamentation and chased. Price, 75c.

No. 62742. Napkin Ring, satin finished, fancy. Price, 90c.

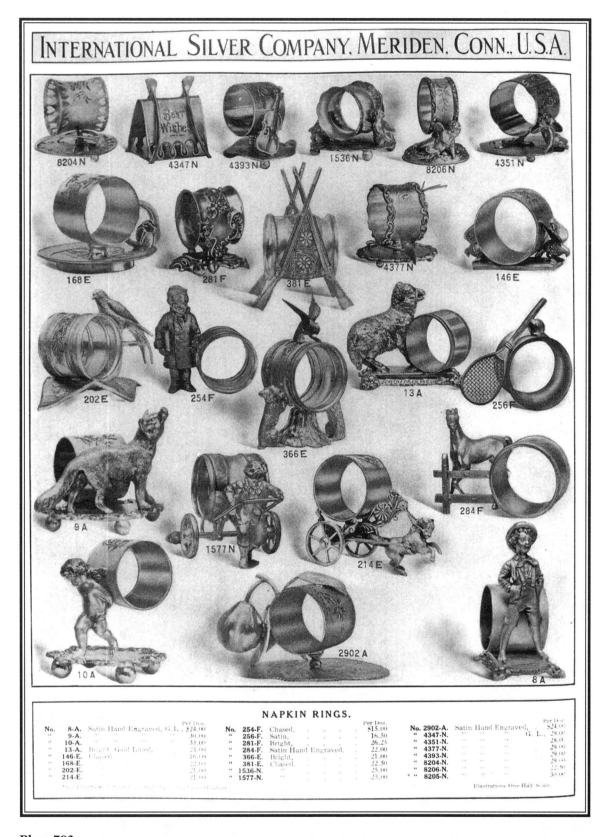

Plate 792

A page from a ca. 1910 International Silver Co. catalog no. 30-1 with illustrations showing napkin rings from the following companies, which merged to form International: Barbour Silver Co., Meriden Britannia Co., Meriden Silver Plate Co., and Wilcox Silver Plate Co.

Plate 793

A page from a ca. 1910 International Silver Co. catalog no. 30-1, which shows the factories of some of the companies which formed International. Clockwise from top center, Derby Silver Co., Wilcox Silver Plate Co., Simpson Nickel Co., Rogers & Brother, The Norwich Cutlery Co., The Watrous Mfg. Co., Wm. Rogers Mfg. Co., and Barbour Silver Co. The three center factories under Derby are Holmes & Edwards, Meriden Britannia Co., and Simpson, Hall, Miller & Co.

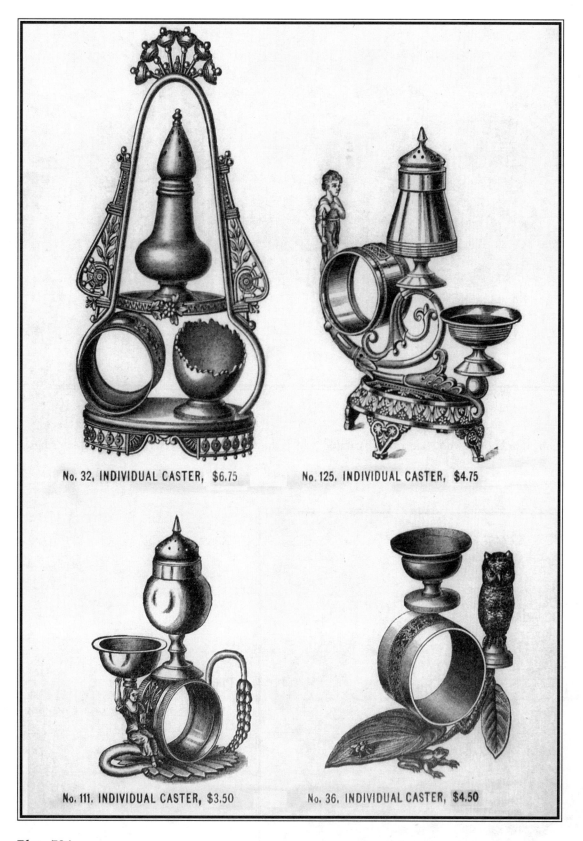

Plate 794

A page from the 1885 catalog of W. H. McCausland, Phillipsburg, Pennsylvania.

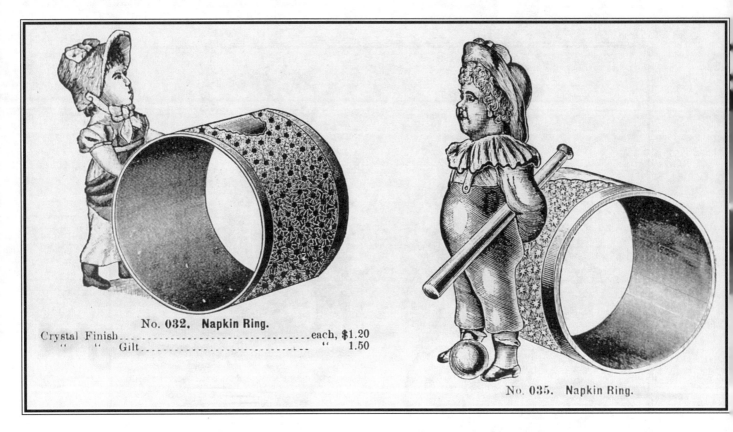

No. 032. Napkin Ring.

Crystal Finish...each, $1.20
"   "   Gilt.."   1.50

No. 035. Napkin Ring.

Plate 795

An illustration from an unknown, wholesale jobber's catalog, which shows two Kate Greenaway-type napkin rings.

No. 68. Napkin Ring.

Bright Cut ....each, $1.42

Plate 796

An artist's illustration of a Pairpoint Manufacturing Co. napkin ring.

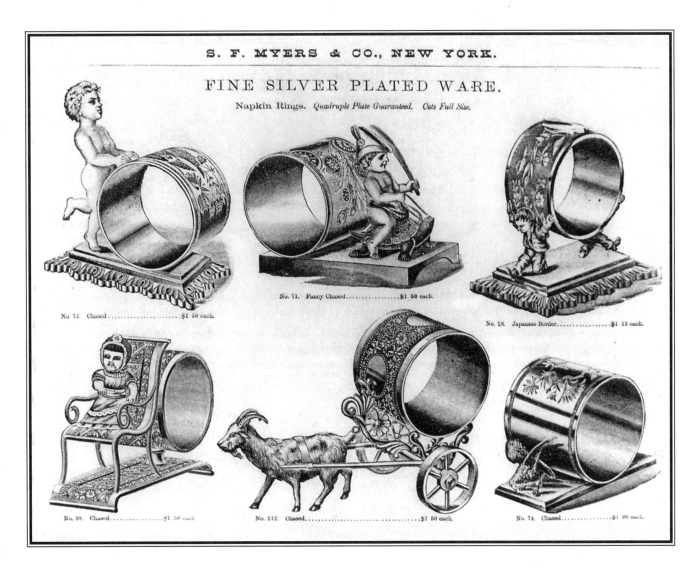

Plate 797

A catalog page, which illustrates napkin rings by Middletown Plate Co. and Meriden Britannia Co.

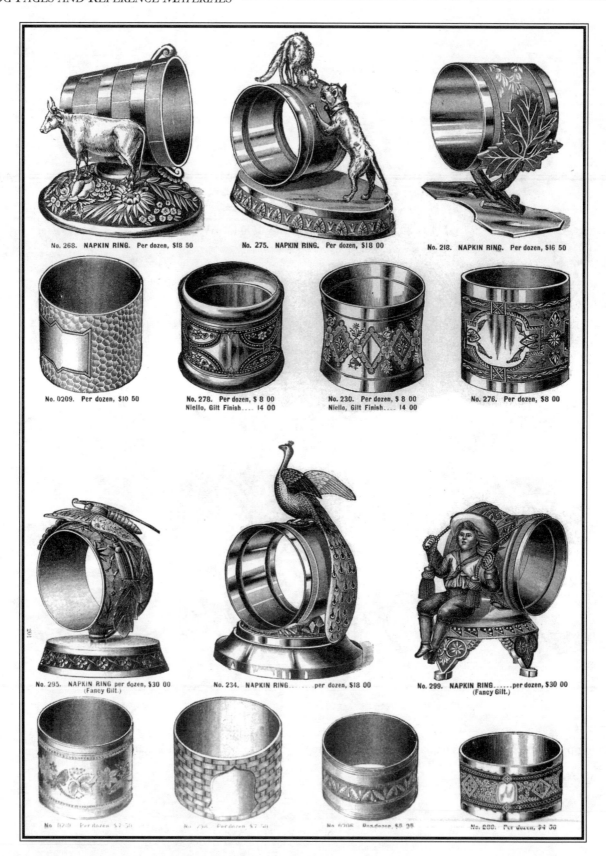

No. 268. NAPKIN RING. Per dozen, $18 50

No. 275. NAPKIN RING. Per dozen, $18 00

No. 218. NAPKIN RING. Per dozen, $16 50

No. 0209. Per dozen, $10 50

No. 278. Per dozen, $ 8 00
Niello, Gilt Finish.... 14 00

No. 230. Per dozen, $ 8 00
Niello, Gilt Finish.... 14 00

No. 276. Per dozen, $8 00

No. 295. NAPKIN RING per dozen, $30 00
(Fancy Gilt.)

No. 234. NAPKIN RING........per dozen, $18 00

No. 299. NAPKIN RING......per dozen, $30 00
(Fancy Gilt.)

No. 0210. Per dozen, $7 50

No. 750. Per dozen, $7 50

No. 0206. Per dozen, $5 25

No. 280. Per dozen, $4 50

Plate 798

A page from an unknown, wholesale jobber's catalog.

No. 144. COMBINATION CASTER.
Silver and Gilt, $6 50.

No. 159. COMBINATION CASTER.
Silver and Gilt, $6 75.

No.133. Combination Salt and Ring, $3 50.

No. 125. COMBINATION CASTER.
Salt, Gold Lined, $4 75.

No. 126. COMBINATION CASTER.
Silver and Gilt, $5 50.

Plate 799

A page from an unknown, wholesale jobber's catalog.

Plate 800

An illustration from an 1870s catalog of The Wm. Rogers Mfg. Co.

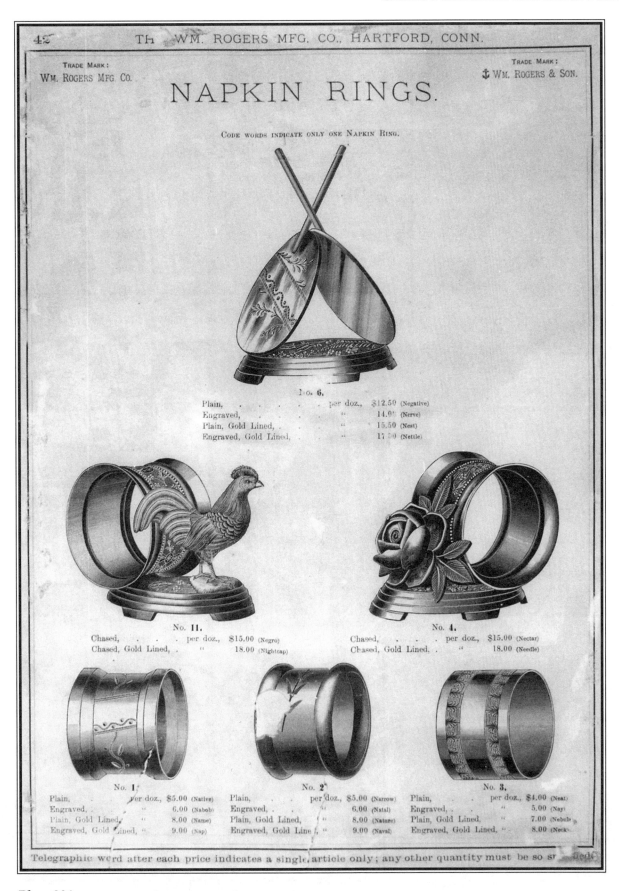

TRADE MARK:
WM. ROGERS MFG. CO.

TRADE MARK:
⚓ WM. ROGERS & SON.

NAPKIN RINGS.

CODE WORDS INDICATE ONLY ONE NAPKIN RING.

No. 6.

Plain,	per doz.,	$12.50	(Negative)
Engraved,	"	14.00	(Nerve)
Plain, Gold Lined,	"	15.50	(Nest)
Engraved, Gold Lined,	"	17.50	(Nettle)

No. 11.

Chased,	per doz.,	$15.00	(Negro)
Chased, Gold Lined,	"	18.00	(Nightcap)

No. 4.

Chased,	per doz.,	$15.00	(Nectar)
Chased, Gold Lined,	"	18.00	(Needle)

No. 1.

Plain,	per doz.,	$5.00	(Native)
Engraved,	"	6.00	(Nabob)
Plain, Gold Lined,	"	8.00	(Name)
Engraved, Gold Lined,	"	9.00	(Nap)

No. 2.

Plain,	per doz.,	$5.00	(Narrow)
Engraved,	"	6.00	(Natal)
Plain, Gold Lined,	"	8.00	(Nature)
Engraved, Gold Lined,	"	9.00	(Naval)

No. 3.

Plain,	per doz.,	$4.00	(Neat)
Engraved,	"	5.00	(Nay)
Plain, Gold Lined,	"	7.00	(Nebula)
Engraved, Gold Lined,	"	8.00	(Neck)

Telegraphic word after each price indicates a single article only; any other quantity must be so specified.

Plate 801

An illustration from an 1870s catalog of The Wm. Rogers Mfg. Co.

No. 57. NAPKIN RING and PEPPER $3.50

Plate 802

An illustration from an unknown, wholesale jobber's catalog.

Plate 803

An illustration from an unknown, wholesale jobber's catalog.

No. 4376. NAPKIN RING .... Each, $2.00

Satin Bright Cut, Raised Border.

No. 312. NAPKIN RING .... Each, $1.75

No. 311. NAPKIN RING [Importune].. ....Each, $1.50

No. 202. NAPKIN RING [Imposition] ....Each, $1.25

Plate 804

An illustration from an unknown, wholesale jobber's catalog.

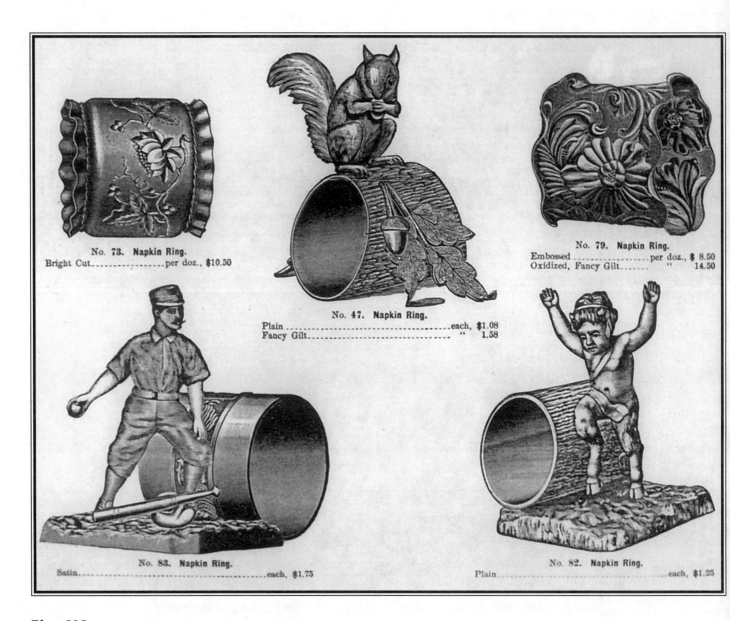

No. 73. Napkin Ring.
Bright Cut.....................per doz., $10.50

No. 47. Napkin Ring.
Plain..................................each, $1.08
Fancy Gilt.............................." 1.58

No. 79. Napkin Ring.
Embossed.....................per doz., $ 8.50
Oxidized, Fancy Gilt........ "   14.50

No. 83. Napkin Ring.
Satin..................................each, $1.75

No. 82. Napkin Ring.
Plain..................................each, $1.25

Plate 805

An illustration from an unknown, wholesale jobber's catalog, which shows Pairpoint Manufacturing Co. napkin rings.

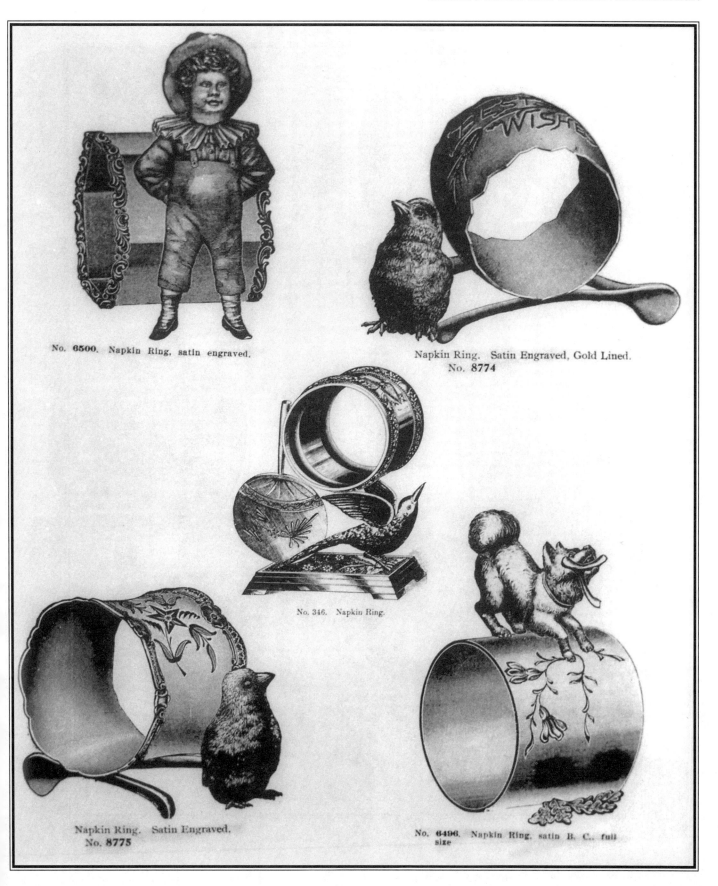

No. **6500**. Napkin Ring, satin engraved.

Napkin Ring. Satin Engraved, Gold Lined.
No. **8774**

No. 346. Napkin Ring.

Napkin Ring. Satin Engraved.
No. **8775**

No. **6496**. Napkin Ring, satin B. C., full size

Plate 806

An illustration from an unknown, wholesale jobber's catalog.

No. 95. Napkin Ring.
Fancy Gilt .... per doz., $18.00
Chased .... " " 9.90

No. 207. Napkin Ring, each, $2.10
Gold-lined .... each, $2.40

No. 84. Napkin Ring.
Embossed .... per doz., $6.50

No. 204. Napkin Ring, each, $2.70
Gold-lined .... each, $3.00

No. 205. Napkin Ring, each, $2.10
Gold-lined .... each, $2.40

No. 209. Napkin Ring, each, $3.00
Gold-lined .... each, $3.30

No. 033. Napkin Ring.
Chased .... each, $1.50
Gold-lined .... " 1.80

No. 04. Napkin Ring.
Chased .... each, $1.69
Gold-lined .... " 1.88

Plate 807

An illustration from an unknown, wholesale jobber's catalog. The napkin rings on this page are primarily by Simpson, Hall, Miller & Co.

No. 24. INDIVIDUAL CASTER $5.75
Gold Lined.

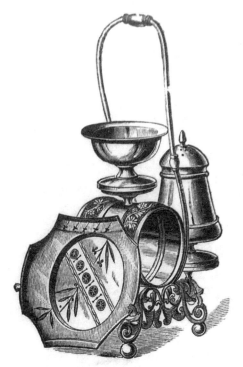

No. 21. INDIVIDUAL CASTER $4.75
Salt, Pepper, Butter Plate and Napkin Ring.

No. 15. INDIVIDUAL CASTER $4.75
Salt, Pepper, Butter Plate, Napkin Ring.

No. 23. INDIVIDUAL CASTER $4.75
Salt, Pepper, Butter Plate, Napkin Ring.

Plate 808

An illustration from an unknown, wholesale jobber's catalog.

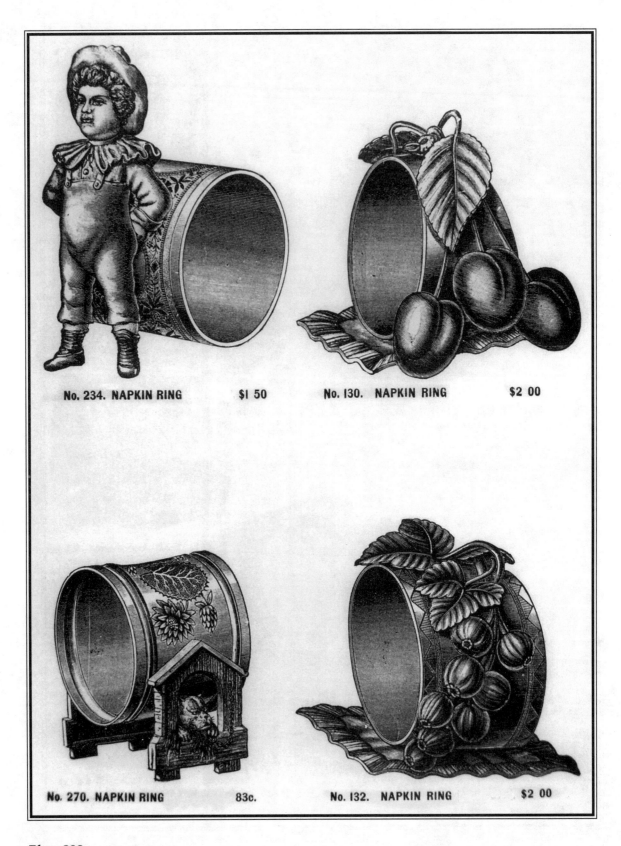

Plate 809

An illustration from an unknown, wholesale jobber's catalog.

No. 6494. Napkin Ring, satin, B. C., gold lined

No. 6510. Napkin Ring, burnished.

No. 6501. Napkin Ring, satin engraved,

No. 6498. Napkin Ring, satin B. C.,

No. 6497. Napkin Ring, silver,

No. 6502. Napkin Ring, satin engraved,

Plate 810

An illustration from an unknown, wholesale jobber's catalog.

No. 284.   Each, $2.25   No. 283.   Each, $2.25

No. 282.   Each, $1.38   No. 137.   Each, $1.00
                                     Satin Bright Cut.

Plate 811

An illustration from an unknown, wholesale jobber's catalog.

No. 9. Combination Set.

Chased, Gilt $7.20

No. 5. Combination Set.

Chased, Gilt $6.60

No. 024. Napkin Ring.

Chased $2.40
Chased, Gilt 2.70
Chased, Fancy Gilt 8.00

No. 7. Combination Set.

Fine Cut Glass Bottles, Gilt $3.10

Plate 812

An illustration from an unknown, wholesale jobber's catalog.

Plate 813

An illustration from an unknown, wholesale jobber's catalog.

No. 96. Napkin Ring, Chased. .$16 00 per doz.

No. 68. Napkin Ring, Chased. .$18 00 per doz.

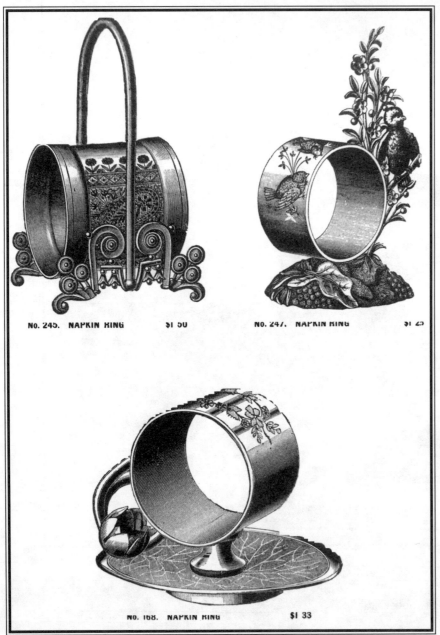

NO. 245. NAPKIN RING $1 50

NO. 247. NAPKIN RING $1 25

NO. 168. NAPKIN RING $1 33

Plate 814

An illustration from an unknown, wholesale jobber's catalog.

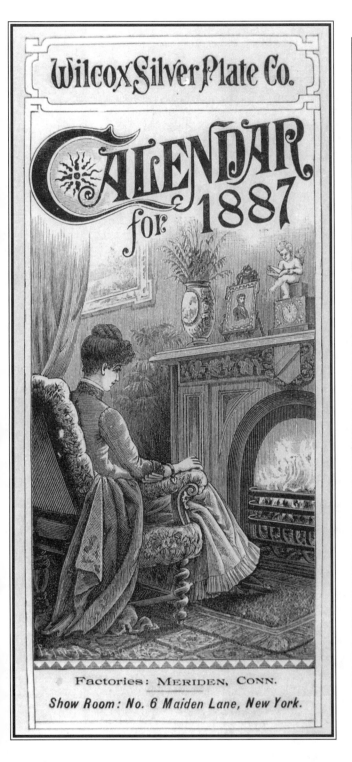

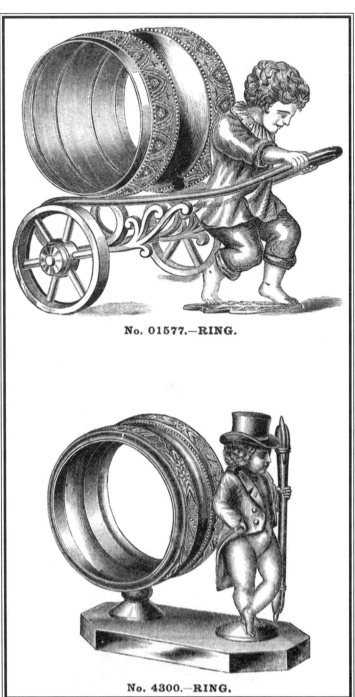

No. 01577.—RING.

No. 4300.—RING.

Plate 815

This illustration shows the front cover of a free advertising calendar, which was distributed by Wilcox Silver Plate Co. in 1887. Each month featured a different example of goods produced by the company.

Plate 816

The month of September featured these napkin rings produced by Wilcox Silver Plate Co.

The following photographs show seven pages from the Meriden Silver Plate Co., ca. 1879 catalog of photograph paste-ups. This is a preliminary process used by manufacturers to provide a layout for the printer in the production of its wholesale catalog.

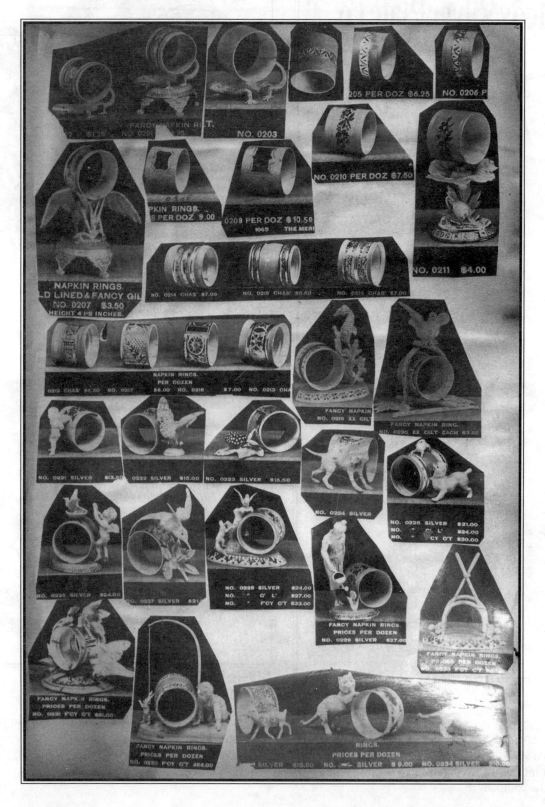

Plate 817

Plate 818

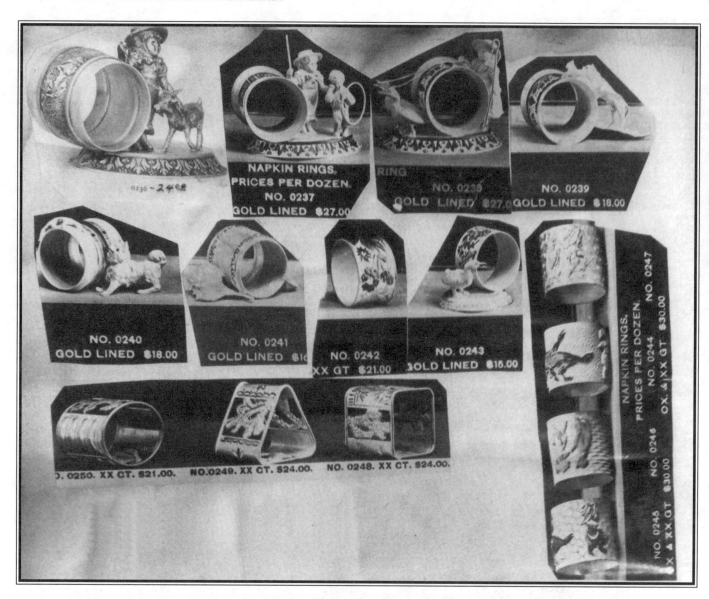

Plate 819

Plate 820

Plate 821

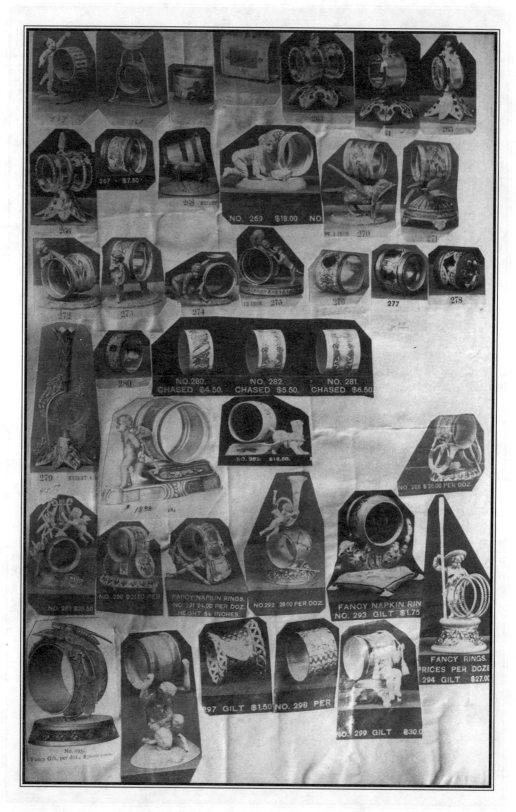

Plate 822

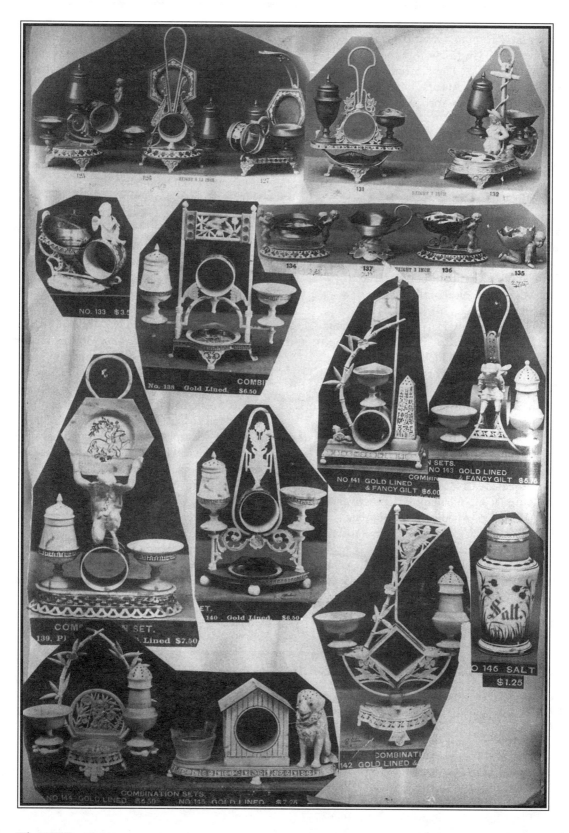

Plate 823

MANUFACTURERS AND MERCHANDISERS

Acme Silver Co., Toronto, Ontario, Canada
Adelphi Silver Plate Co., New York, New York
Anchor Silver Plate Co., Muncie, Indiana
Aurora Silver Plate Co., Aurora, Illinois
J. A. Babcock & Co., New York, New York
Bailey & Brainard
Barbour Bros. Co., Hartford, Connecticut
Barbour Silver Co., Hartford, Connecticut
R. Barrie, Chelsea, Massachusetts
Bridgeport Silver Co., Bridgeport, Connecticut
Deerpark Mfg. Co.
Derby Silver Co., Birmingham, Connecticut
Forbes Silver Co., Meriden, Connecticut
A. Frankfield & Co.
Hall, Elton & Co., Wallingford, Connecticut
Chas. W. Hamill & Co., Baltimore, Maryland
Hamilton Mfg. Co., Chicago, Illinois
Hamilton Silver Co., New York, New York
Hartford Silver Plate Co., Hartford, Connecticut
Holmes & Edwards Silver Co., Bridgeport, Connecticut
Homan Silver Plate Co., Cincinnati, Ohio
Knickerbocker Silver Co., Port Jervis, New York
A. Ledig & Son
Manhattan Silver Plate Co., Brooklyn, New York
    (later Lyons, New York)
Manning, Bowman & Co., Meriden, Connecticut
Meriden Britannia Co., Meriden, Connecticut
Meriden Britannia Co., Hamilton, Ontario, Canada
Meriden Silver Plate Co., Meriden, Connecticut
Meyer & Warne Co., Philadelphia, Pennsylvania
Middletown Plate Co., Middletown, Connecticut
New Haven Silver Plate Co., Lyons, New York
Osborn & Co., Lancaster, Pennsylvania
Thomas Otley & Sons [Sheffield]
Pairpoint Manufacturing Co., New Bedford, Massachusetts

Pelton Bros. & Co., St. Louis, Missouri
Philadelphia Plate Co., Philadelphia, Pennsylvania
Poole Silver Co., Taunton, Massachusetts
Queen City Silver Co., Cincinnati, Ohio
Racine Silver Plate Co., Racine, Wisconsin
Reed & Barton, Taunton, Massachusetts
Rockford Silver Plate Co., Rockford, Illinois
Rogers & Brother, Waterbury, Connecticut
Roger, Smith & Co., Hartford, Connecticut (later New Haven, Connecticut)
Wm. A. Rogers, Ltd., Ontario, Canada
Wm. Rogers Mfg. Co., Hartford, Connecticut
F. B. Rogers Silver Co., Shelburne Falls, Massachusetts, in 1883, (Taunton, Massachusetts in 1886)
Wm. Rogers & Son, Hartford, Connecticut
Henry Schade, Brooklyn, New York
I. J. Sharick, Albuquerque, New Mexico
Simons & Miller Plate Co., Middletown, Connecticut
Simpson, Hall, Miller & Co., Wallingford, Connecticut
Simpson, Hall, Miller & Co., Montreal, Canada
Southington Cutlery Co., Southington, Connecticut
Southington Silver Plate Co., Southington, Connecticut
Standard Silver Co., Ltd., Toronto, Canada
Stix & L'Allemand, New York
Strickland & Co., Albany, New York
Taunton Silverplate Co., Taunton, Massachusetts
Toronto Silver Plate Co., Toronto, Canada
James W. Tufts, Boston, Massachusetts
Van Bergh Silver Plate Co., Rochester, New York
Victor Silver Co., Birmingham, Connecticut
E. G. Webster & Bro., Brooklyn, New York
Webster Mfg. Co., Brooklyn, New York
E. G. Webster & Son, Brooklyn, New York
West Silver Co., Taunton, Massachusetts
Wilcox Silver Plate Co., Meriden, Connecticut
Winsted Silver Plate Co.

PHOTO CREDITS

Richard Goodbar writes and lectures on the decorative arts, but his major interest is English silver. His photographs have appeared in many publications, including *Silver in Maryland* by Jennifer Goldsborough and published by The Maryland Historical Society, and the *Magazine Antiques.* Mr Goodbar's articles, accompanied by his photographs, have appeared in the *Maine Antiques Digest*, *The Lapidary Journal*, and catalogs of many antiques shows in Maryland. Mr. Goodbar currently serves on the Baltimore Museum of Art's Decorative Arts Accession Committee.

BIBLIOGRAPHY

Books

Bishop, Robert. *American Folk Sculpture.* New York: E. P. Dutton & Co., Inc., 1974.

Bishop, Robert, and Patricia Coblentz. *A Gallery of American Weathervanes and Whirligigs.* New York: Bonanza Books, 1981.

Book of North American Birds. Pleasantville, New York: Reader's Digest Association, Inc., 1990.

Fleming, John, and Hugh Honour. *Dictionary of the Decorative Arts.* New York: Harper & Row, 1977.

Freeman, Larry, and Jane Beaumont. *Early American Plated Silver.* Watkins Glen, New York: Century House, 1947.

Fried, Frederick. *Artists in Wood.* New York: Bramhall House, 1970.

Hogan, Edmund P. *The Elegance of Old Silverplate.* Exton, Pennsylvania: Schiffer Publishing, Limited, 1980.

Miller, Steve. *The Art of the Weathervane.* Exton, Pennsylvania: Schiffer Publishing, Ltd., 1984.

New Larousse *Encyclopedia of Mythology.* London: Hamlyn Publishing Group, Ltd., 1959.

Rainwater, Dorothy. *Encyclopedia of American Silver Manufacturers.* 3rd rev. ed. Exton, Pennsylvania: Schiffer Publishing, Ltd., 1986.

Rainwater, Dorothy T. and H. Ivan. *American Silverplate.* West Chester, Pennsylvania: Schiffer Publishing, Ltd., 1988.

Schnadig, Victor K. *American Victorian Figural Napkin Rings.* Des Moines, Iowa: Wallace-Homestead Book Company, 1971.

Stafford, Maureen, and Dora Ware. *An Illustrated Dictionary of Ornament.* London: George Allen & Unwin, Ltd., 1974.

Sterling Silver, Silverplate and Souvenir Spoons with Prices. Gas City, Indiana: L-W, Inc., 1977.

The Oxford Companion to the Decorative Arts. Edited by Harold Osborne. London: Oxford at the Clarendon Press, Oxford University Press, 1975.

Unitt, Doris and Peter. *Canadian Silver, Silver Plate & Related Glass.* Ontario: Clock House, 1970.

Victorian Silverplated Holloware. Princeton, New Jersey: ed. The Pyne Press, 1972.

Catalogs

Early Original Catalogs, Flyers, and Advertisements. Some are reprints. They include:

Benjamin Allen & Co., Chicago, (a jobber of clocks and watches). Original 1893 Catalog titled Busiest House in America.

Selections from the W. G. Crook's (Nelsonville, Ohio) Illustrated. Catalogue of 1888. Busiest House in America. Reprinted in 1972 by Collector's Weekly, Kermit, Texas.

International Silver Co. Catalog No. 30-1, ca. 1910, Meriden, Connecticut.

W. H. McCausland. Phillipsburg, Pennsylvania. Busiest House in America, 1885.

The Meriden Britannia Silverplate Treasury. 1886-7 catalog, by The Meriden Britannia Co. New York: Dover Publications, 1982. S. F. Myers & Co., New York.

Pairpoint Manufacturing Co. 1894 catalog. Washington Mills, New York: The Gilded Age Press, 1979.

The Toronto Silver Plate Co.'s Illustrated Catalogue and Price List of Electro Silver Plate. Toronto, Canada, 1888. Peterborough, Ontario: Clock House Publications, 1977.

Catalogue of Otto Young & Co., Chicago, 1884. (Western Agents for Meriden Silver Plate Co..)

Original Catalogs

Barbour Silver Co., ca. 1880
Derby Silver Co., 1883
Forbes Silver Co., 1913–14
Meriden Britannia Co., 1878, 1890
Meriden Silver Plate Co., 1879
Middletown Plate Co., 1879, 1892–93
Reed & Barton, 1877, 1885
The Wm. Rogers Mfg. Co., ca. 1870
Henry Schade, ca. 1880
Sears, Roebuck and Co., 1897
Simpson, Hall, Miller & Co., 1878, 1882, 1886, 1887–88, 1891
James W. Tufts, ca. 1880
E. G. Webster & Bro., 1884
Wilcox Silver Plate Co., ca. 1886

Magazines

Silver Magazine, Whittier, California
Vol. IV, No. 2, March–April, 1971
Vol. IV, No. 3, May–June, 1971
Vol. XXIV, No. V, September–October, 1991
Vol. XXIV, No. VI, November–December, 1991
Vol. XXV, No. I, January–February, 1992
Vol. XXV, No. II, March–April, 1992
Vol. XXV, No. IV, July–August, 1992

Articles

Bronow, Ron. "Reproductions of American Victorian Silver-plated Figural Napkin Rings." *Maine Antique Digest*, May 1984.

Other Sources

Wilcox Silver Plate Co., Meriden, Connecticut. Original Calendar for 1887. Month of September.
A scrapbook with seven original pages from a Meriden Silver Plate Co. catalog with illustrations of figural napkin rings.
More information was culled from libraries, old city directories, histories, and sources too numerous to include here.

INDEX

A. C. & CO 83
A. Frankfield & Co 17
A. Ledig & Son 93
Acme Silver Co. 5, 22, 38, 44, 112, 122, 129, 196, 203, 237
Adelphi Silver Plate Co. 289
Anchor Silver Plate Co. 143
Aurora Silver Plate Co........15, 28, 47, 104, 128, 145, 155-156, 173, 176, 179, 203, 240, 271, 280, 285
Baby...............................134
Bailey and Brainard..................137
Barbour Bros. Co. 201
Barbour Silver Co. 46, 57, 73, 148, 151, 194, 195, 268, 278, 284, 319-320
Baseball 212
Bee 49, 159
Billiken 142
Bird 19-20, 35, 128-132, 137, 153-157, 160, 163, 166, 171, 176, 179, 188, 191, 261, 268
Bison...............................80
Boars..............................80
Bolts and Wing Nuts..................7
Book..........75, 87, 120, 177, 191, 230, 231, 243-244, 250, 259, 277
Books.............................231
Boy ....161, , 209
Bridgeport Silver Co. 72, 254, 258
Bud vase 162, 258, 316
Butterfly.........129, 131, 134, 145, 152, 155, 169, 178-179, 188, 241
Camel.............................79
Cat 225, 317
Chair..........................207, 230
Chas. W. Hamill & Co. 34
Cherries...........................241
Cherub 126, 154, 157, 172, 315
   with wings 125, 127, 129, 132, 152, 156, 158, 171, 173
Chicken............................149
Clown.............................141
Conquistador 159
Court jester.....................145-146
Cupid 157
Deerpark Mfg. Co. 39
Derby Silver Co.......16, 31, 42, 55, 67, 85, 86, 87, 113, 114, 119, 134, 177, 200-201, 207, 215, 222, 226-228, 236, 243-244, 250, 254, 256, 267-269, 274, 276, 278, 280, 290-291, 298, 308, 312, 315, 320

Dog 155,170, 179, 193, 214, 217-218, 222-223, 227-228, 235, 267, 271
Dolphin.......................164, 182
E. & H. Mfg. Co....................176
E.G. Webster & Bro.........82, 92, 105, 107, 123, 130, 151, 168
E.G. Webster & Brother 97, 105
Elephant 77-78
Elves.............................145
F.B. Rogers Silver Co. ..17, 34, 35, 217
Fan 134, 153
Fireman's hat......................248
Flute..............................177
Forbes Silver Co. 40, 211
Fox 33, 163, 181
Frog........................26, 32, 155
Geese.............................224
Giraffe 79-80, 131
Girl...............................172
Gnome............................173
Goat 33, 225
Grading & Pricing...................6
Grapes............................191
Greenaway, Kate ...147, 148, 169, 292-294, 297, 304, 306, 310, 313, 322
Hall, Elton & Co. 181
Hamilton Silver Co. 48
Hartford Silver Plate Co. 14, 121, 131, 148, 151, 194, 196, 213, 314
Henry Schade 140
Holmes & Edwards Silver Co..160, 320
Homan Silver Plate Co. 35, 55, 141, 146, 228
Horse.......................33, 124, 210
Horseshoe ...30, 44, 104, 251, 252, 291
Infant.............................258
International Silver Co. 5, 108, 319-320
J. A. Babcock & Co.......39, 44, 96, 225
Jack and Jill 232
James W. Tufts....52, 59, 61, 74, 78, 98, 124, 149, 161, 175, 177, 179, 188, 212
Kangaroo..........................76
Kewpie 303
Knickerbocker Silver Co. 9-10, 37, 39, 71, 77, 140
Knight............................140
Little Red Riding Hood 139
Lizard 76-77
Lyre..............................176
M.W.C. 172
Man 131, 156, 168

Manhattan Silver Plate Co. 94, 178
Manning, Bowman & Co. 22, 316
Manufacturers' Marks and Numbers..7
Mary Gregory......................130
Meriden............................112
Meriden Britannia Co. 5, 7-9, 15, 19-20, 29, 37-38, 40, 41, 52, 54, 59, 65, 75, 79, 81, 87-89, 91, 93-94, 101, 104, 106-107, 109, 112-113, 115-118, 127-128, 141, 144, 152-153, 159, 163, 170, 172, 181, 191, 193-194, 197, 199-200, 203-205, 215, 226, 233, 240, 242-243, 246, 250, 255, 263, 270-271, 274-276, 287-292, 301-302, 306, 312, 317, 319-320, 323
Meriden Silver Plate Co. 11, 13, 18, 34, 36, 45-46, 73, 77, 80, 100-103, 106, 114, 116, 140, 145, 154, 160, 166, 180-183, 189-191, 199, 206, 209-210, 224-225, 233, 242, 244-245, 247, 252, 254-256, 260-262, 272, 277, 282-283, 295, 299, 306, 307, 319, 340
Meyer & Warne Co....................172
Middletown Plate Co. ...38, 41, 49, 57, 64, 93, 97, 121, 147-148, 155, 176, 182, 186, 190, 192, 194-195, 204, 206-208, 259, 267, 270, 272, 275, 315, 323
Military 220
Monkey............................318
Mouse.............................10
Music 9, 14, 62-63, 120, 125, 141, 176-177, 180, 190, 216, 220, 231, 241-242, 249, 257, 262, 274, 315
New Haven Silver Plate Co. 238
Osborn & Co. 28, 108, 113, 119
Owl....................148, 167, 217
Pairpoint Manufacturing Co..........20, 67-68, 71, 82-83, 88, 99, 103-104, 108, 129, 141, 143, 153, 164, 177, 188, 201-202, 238-239, 243, 248, 252-253, 259, 291, 303, 309, 322, 330
Palmer Cox Brownie 143, 299
Pelton Bros. & Co. ...56, 102, 139, 241
Philadelphia Plate Co. 56, 69
Poole Silver Co......................315
Queen City Silver Co. 48
R. Barrie.........................162
R. Strickland & Co. 138
Rabbit.......................143, 260

Racine Silver Plate Co........79, 95, 163, 165, 178-179

Rat 192

Reed & Barton   5, 17, 21, 23, 28, 34, 43, 47, 50, 68, 72, 82, 93-95, 101-102, 115, 123, 125-126, 135, 137-139, 145-146, 181, 183-184, 186, 193, 217, 241-242, 244, 257, 261-262, 266, 272, 281-282, 285, 289, 309, 317

Rip Van Winkle 142

Rockford Silver Plate Co.   25, 52-53, 79, 88-89, 91, 98, 128-129, 131, 133, 150, 162-163, 174, 179, 187, 219, 253

Rogers & Brother 7, 10, 70, 76, 80, 87, 105, 108, 120, 125, 155, 180, 182, 200, 243, 279, 320

Rogers, Smith & Co. 20, 32, 75, 79, 90, 92, 94, 117, 120, 132, 161, 166, 190, 199, 212, 215, 224, 250, 255, 287, 310-311

Sailor........125, 154, 210, 272-273, 317

Satyr 140

Schade, Henry 43, 106

Sharick, I.J.....................................255

Silver Plating...6

Simons & Miller Plate Co. 138

Simpson, Hall, Miller & Co. ..5, 7, 21-22, 26-27, 29, 31, 44, 53, 67, 75, 83, 91, 99, 111, 112, 115, 122, 123, 134, 142, 146, 154, 157-158, 165-166, 171-172, 180, 184, 188, 191, 200, 203, 210, 211, 216-218, 220-221, 229-232, 235, 254, 256, 273, 281, 292, 300, 304, 306, 320, 332

Sled 38, 50, 53, 110, 181, 229, 265, 292, 294, 308

Southington Cutlery Co......66, 77, 84, 158, 233, 238-239, 279, 284, 286

Southington Silver Plate Co...........275

Sphinx 144

Standard Silver Co. 112, 196-197

Stewart & Jones 310

Stix and L'Allemand.......................288

Swan 150, 179, 190

Taunton Silverplate Co. 123-124, 152, 156, 159, 165

Thomas Otley & Sons....................135

Toronto Silver Plate Co.......42, 50, 51, 53, 59, 72, 100, 111-112, 121, 148, 151, 168, 191, 194-196, 204-205, 208, 218, 222, 231, 237, 239, 247, 251, 269, 277, 308, 314

Triton 144

Tufts, James W. 9, 11, 16-17, 21, 23, 90, 113, 156, 171, 198, 209, 213-214, 216, 223, 229, 232, 234-235, 251-253, 255, 258-259, 281, 293, 297, 299, 301-302, 304-305, 308, 310, 313

Turtle 134, 182, 192

Van Bergh Silver Plate Co.........66, 73 110, 187, 192, 28(

Victor Silver Co. ....31, 6?

Wagon...17?

Webster Mfg. Co. ....24, 33, 54, 8?

West Silver Co. ....133, 169, 29?

Wheels......29, 38, 41-42, 86, 110, 117 169-172, 174, 185, 197, 208, 221 222, 243-244, 253, 264-265, 26! 269, 300, 31?

Wilcox Silver Plate Co. ...5, 12-13, 21? 22, 26, 36, 56, 60, 61, 69, 76, 10? 110, 111, 119, 131, 149-150, 15? 162, 164, 167, 174-176, 178, 18(183, 185, 187, 191, 223, 236, 24? 257, 263-265, 276, 284, 292, 29? 316, 319-320, 33?

William Rogers Mfg. Co. ....2?

Winsted Silver Plate Co. ....25(

Wm. Rogers & Co............................12(

Wm. Rogers & Son ....24, 256, 27?

Wm. Rogers Mfg. Co. .....7, 18, 29-30 55, 80, 96, 109, 133, 169, 20? 204, 218-219, 257, 266-268, 27? 286, 305, 320, 326-32?

WMF ....3(

Woman ....133, 146, 159-160, 17?

Lillian Gottschalk is an award-winning author of *American Toy Cars & Trucks*. Antiques have been her lifelong interest. A former feature writer covering stories on antiques, her articles have appeared in *The Maine Antique Digest*, *Automobile Quarterly*, *Encyclopedia of Collectibles*, *Time-Life Books*, *The Antique Toy World Magazine*, and other publications. Since 1953, she has been a collector of American Victorian figural napkin rings. She resides in Parkton, Maryland.

Sandra Whitson grew up in the world of antiques. Her father, Frank G. Whitson, was an antiques dealer in Baltimore, Maryland, for 46 years, and it was he who instilled in Sandra a love of collecting. She began her figural napkin ring collection 25 years ago. When she married California antiques dealer Ron Van Anda, her avocation also became her vocation. Today, she travels the U.S. buying and selling figural napkin rings. In 1990, Sandra published a feature article about her patriotic rhinestone jewelry collection in *The Inside Collector* magazine. She and her husband reside in Lititz, Pennsylvania.